# Insurance Law

# ■ EUROPEAN LAW SERIES ■

*Series Editor:*
**PROFESSOR JOHN A. USHER**

# EC Insurance Law

ROBERT MERKIN
Professor of Commercial Law,
Cardiff Law School

and

ANGUS RODGER
Solicitor, Clifford Chance, London

LONGMAN
LONDON AND NEW YORK

Addison Wesley Longman
Edinburgh Gate
Harlow
Essex CM20 2JE
England
*and Associated Companies throughout the world.*

*Published in the United States of America
by Addison Wesley Longman Inc., New York.*

First published 1997

ISBN 0 582 28719 7 PPR

**British Library Cataloguing-in-Publication Data**

A catalogue record of this book is
available from the British Library

**Library of Congress Cataloging-in-Publication Data**

A catalog entry for this title is available from the
Library of Congress

Transferred to digital print on demand 2001

Printed and bound by Antony Rowe Ltd, Eastbourne

# Contents

# Preface

We are indebted to the following individuals for their advice on foreign law: Laurent Legein (Belgium), Françoise Blum and Gilles Heude (France), Johannes Kremer (Germany), Alessandro Bozza (Italy), Graham Wladimiroff (Netherlands) and Sonsoles Seoane (Spain). We would also like to thank Paulino Pereira of the EC Secretariat-General and Manuel De Frutos and Yvette Chrissantonis of DG XV who have patiently answered various queries.

The law is stated as known to us at 1 January 1997. The text and appendixes take account of the conventions for the accession of Austria, Finland and Sweden to the Brussels and Rome Conventions.

Robert Merkin and
Angus Rodger
March 1997

# General Editor's Preface

The Longman European Law Series is the first comprehensive series of topic-based books on EC Law aimed primarily at a student readership, though I have no doubt that they will also be found useful by academic colleagues and interested practitioners. It has become more and more difficult for a single course or a single book to deal comprehensively with all the major topics of Community law, and the intention of this series is to enable students and teachers to 'mix and match' topics which they find to be of interest; it may also be hoped that the publication of this series will encourage the study of areas of Community law which have historically been neglected in degree courses. However, while the series may have a student readership in mind, the authors have been encouraged to take an academic and critical approach, placing each topic in its overall Community context, and also in its socio-economic and political context where relevant.

There has long been Community legislation in the insurance sector, but it was also an important feature of the programme to complete the internal market by the end of 1992. Robert Merkin and Angus Rodger take the internal market as their starting point, but also look at individual aspects of insurance law which are subject to specific Community legislation. Since this legislation largely takes the form of harmonising Directives, a clear illustration is given of the way in which domestic law has been amended to meet Community obligations (and even proposals). Insurance is also a matter which is given special treatment in the Conventions between the EC Member States on Jurisdiction and Judgments and on Contractual Obligations, and this also is reflected in the book. The authors have presented this complex information in a clear and accessible manner, and in the context of this series show clearly how a highly-developed area of domestic law may be effected by Community requirements.

John A. Usher

# Foreword

By *Professor Walter van Gerven*
*Advocate General, Court of Justice of the*
*European Communities 1988–94*
*Professor of Law, Katholieke Universiteit Leuven*

A special feature of the *European Law Series* is its aim to provide an overview of themes which span very different parts of Community law. Thus this book on EC insurance law explains the many EC directives (and proposals) relating to insurance contracts, motor insurance, insurance intermediaries and the creation of the single market in insurance.

Moreover, it also deals extensively with general Community law rules which have an impact on insurance and reinsurance law, including the Brussels Convention on Jurisdiction and the Enforcement of Judgments in Civil and Commercial Matters, the Rome Convention on the Law Applicable to Contractual Obligations (as well as the special choice of law provisions in the direct insurance directives), the Unfair Contract Terms Directive and the rules on competition. As well as considering the specific insurance provisions of these rules the book gives an overview of the general rules, which makes it of interest to those who are considering the wider context beyond the field of insurance law.

Equally remarkable is the way in which the authors situate Community law instruments against the background of national law, in this case UK law, as it stood before the arrival of Community law. They then discuss, in a most informative way, how Community law has been implemented in domestic law and, in a wider context, how domestic law has been influenced by Community law.

The book is not only of interest to readers from the UK. The excellent explanation of complicated Community regulations will help readers from other EC countries to understand Community law. The many decisions of the English courts and the European Court of Justice will assist readers from other EC countries to interpret the Brussels and Rome Conventions. And from the comparative perspective the book provides a useful insight into UK insurance law.

The authors have been able to present a technical subject in such a way that it will be of value both to specialists and to those who deal only occasionally with matters of insurance law. The book is an outstanding contribution to EC insurance law, and to EC law in general.

Walter van Gerven
Leuven

January 1997

# Table of Cases

# Table of Legislation

# Table of Treaties, Conventions and International Agreements

# CHAPTER ONE

# The single insurance market

## The concept of a single market for insurance

The eventual establishment of a single market for insurance within the EC was inherent in the Treaty of Rome itself. Article 52 – the right of establishment – confers the right on a national of a member state to set up a branch, agency or establishment in any other member state without being subjected to restrictions by the host state. Article 59 – the free movement of services – requires member states to abolish restrictions on the provision of services across national boundaries. Translated into the insurance context, these two freedoms implied the twin rights of an EC insurer to: (a) establish itself in any other member state in order to sell insurance within that state; (b) sell insurance to assureds located in any EC member state from an establishment elsewhere in the EC by way of services.

The machinery necessary to achieve a single market for insurance in these respects was scheduled to be put into place on 1 July 1994, the due date for national implementation of the third and final tranche of insurance Directives. Under these Directives, an insurer established and authorised in its home state is free to become established, and to sell insurance by way of services, in any other member state while under the supervision solely of its home authorities, a concept which has become known as the 'Single European Licence'. The process took nearly 30 years to complete.

The reasons for the delay are readily explicable. Insurance, which has as its objectives the spreading of risk and loss, is one of the most important forms of economic activity. Businesses rely upon insurance to protect their assets and to enable them to undertake new ventures which are too speculative for them to risk unprotected exposure. Consumers rely upon insurance to safeguard their possessions and to plan their future income levels. The two categories of person most at risk of personal injury – employees and road users – depend upon employers and drivers being insured against liability incurred. Insurance is also an important source of foreign earnings for many EC countries. However, insurance is also a difficult activity to conduct successfully, as the process of underwriting should involve a deep knowledge of markets, probabilities and statistics: indeed, the history of insurance throughout the world is characterised by regular, and on occasion spectacular, failures of insurance companies.

The extent to which insurance underpins most social and business activities in modern economies, coupled with the need for expertise amongst insurers, has led to detailed financial and related regulation of insurance activity throughout the world. The form of regulation adopted varies from place to place, but perhaps the elements found most commonly are the following.

(a) Administrative authorisation of persons wishing to carry on the insurance activity, to ensure that the insurer's controllers are competent and possess the necessary expertise and that the insurer's business plans will enable it to meet its liabilities to assureds. Prior authorisation is an almost universal feature of national insurance regulation.

(b) Regulation of the solvency of insurers. One of the earliest illustrations is the UK, which, in the Life Assurance Companies Act 1870 adopted a deposit system, whereby an insurer wishing to offer life assurance had to make a financial deposit with the Board of Trade, a sum which could be used to pay assureds in the event of the insurer's failure.

(c) Post-authorisation supervision of insurers, to ensure, inter alia, that the company does not fall into the hands of persons ill-equipped to carry on insurance business and that solvency is maintained.

(d) 'Material control' of insurers, which consists of prior approval of policy terms and premium levels: in some instances, statutory non-excludable policy terms are set out in domestic legislation.

The difficulty facing the European Commission when it embarked upon its single insurance market programme in the 1960s, was that the form of regulation within each member state was different in terms of scope and rigidity. The UK, for example, unlike most Continental jurisdictions, has never accepted the concept of material control as a general principle,[1] and has taken the view that the law should do no more than guarantee that an insurer can afford to pay claims rather than to go further and require payment of particular classes of loss. Consequently, if a single market for insurance, allowing unimpeded cross-border sales and establishment by means of a Single European Licence, was to be created, it was also necessary for a common regulatory regime to be established, so that an insurer seeking to expand from its own territory would not face any additional obligations in the member state which was to be the target of its activities. Equally, from the host state's point of view, the host would have to be sure that an insurer trading in its territory without interference from domestic regulatory authorities was properly supervised in its own member state, and the host would want some form of fall-back supervisory power where the insurer's home state regulators did not fulfil their role adequately. The history of the EC's single market programme is one of compromise and caution.

The Single Insurance Market was achieved by means of three 'generations' of insurance Directives: the first generation was concerned with the right of establishment; the second generation dealt with freedom to provide insurance by way of services; and the third generation converted these two basic principles into the single market. Each generation of Directives treated non-life and life insurance separately, largely for the reason that life insurance was more heavily regulated within the member states, and indeed the Commission tackled the non-life market first, with the life market following on some years behind. Successive generations of Directives took effect partly as legislation in their own right and partly as amendments to earlier generations of Directives: the result proved to be a complex mass of amended and reamended legislation in respect of which there was no authoritative consolidated text. The Commission has announced its intention of consolidating the existing Directives during the course of 1996, although as of September 1996 the draft of the consolidation had not been published.

---

[1.] There are isolated exceptions, the most important being the Road Traffic Act 1988 and the Employers' Liability (Compulsory Insurance) Act 1969, both of which place limits on insurers' contractual defences. The former, which is now based on EC Motor Insurance Directives, is discussed in chapter 3.

At least one modification to the existing structure is contemplated. The Commission proposed, early in 1996, an amendment to the Directives under which, in order to assist regulation, financial transparency would be demanded of a group of companies including an insurance company. The proposals have yet to appear in final form.

# The creation of the single market for insurance

## The Reinsurance Directive

The liberalisation of the insurance market was a stated aim of the Commission in its General Programme on free movement of services drawn up in 1961. The first tentative moves towards the single market were taken in the Reinsurance Directive 1964,[2] this being a relatively simple target given that reinsurance is in many countries significantly less heavily regulated than direct insurance.[3] The Directive required those member states which imposed restrictions on the right of establishment and the freedom to provide services in the reinsurance field to abolish the restrictions and thereby to remove discrimination. EC-based reinsurers were thus given the right to set up branches in other member states and to sell insurance in other member states, in both cases subject to their complying with the host's domestic rules applicable to reinsurers.

## The 'First Generation' Insurance Directives

### Non-life insurance

The First Non-Life Directive of 1973[4] applied to most forms of non-life insurance (art 2 and Annex), the most important exclusion

---

[2.] Council Directive 62/225 of 25 February 1964 on the abolition of restrictions on freedom of establishment and freedom to provide services in respect of reinsurance and retrocession.

[3.] Indeed, it has only recently been confirmed in the UK that reinsurance is the same as insurance for regulatory purposes: *Re NRG Victory Reinsurance Ltd* [1995] 1 All ER 533.

[4.] Council Directive 73/239 of 24 July 1973 on the co-ordination of laws, regulations and administrative provisions relating to the taking-up and pursuit of the business of direct insurance other than life assurance, as amended by Council Directive 76/580 of 29 June 1976 (of the same title) which was concerned purely with defining units of account for currency conversion purposes.

being motor insurance which was compulsory in most member states and which was subjected to substantive as well as regulatory harmonisation in later years. The primary objective of the Directive was to lay down a common regulatory structure for non-life insurers, thereby facilitating the abolition of national restrictions on the right of an insurer established in one member state to become established in another member state. Freedom of establishment for non-life insurers was indeed provided for in a parallel Directive adopted on the same day,[5] which required member states to allow insurers to become established without discrimination on grounds of nationality. The result, therefore, was a structure under which an insurer established in any one state could become established in any other state, providing that the insurer complied with the regulatory rules of the host, those rules to a large extent being harmonised so that an insurer satisfying the requirements of its home state would almost certainly satisfy the requirements for becoming established elsewhere.

The most important regulatory features of the First Non-Life Directive were as follows.

(a) An insurer wishing to carry on insurance business in any member state via any form of establishment was required to obtain prior authorisation from the regulatory authorities of that state, separate authorisation being required for each of the then seventeen classes of business indicated in the Directive (art 6). The Directive required member states to demand a scheme of operations from the insurer, setting out its business plan, financial resources, general and special policy terms and anticipated levels of premium income (art 9). Member states were permitted to impose additional requirements, e.g., on the qualifications of controllers, provided that this was done in a non-discriminatory fashion. The Directive provided also for withdrawal of authorisation where an insurer had failed to comply with conditions for authorisation or with the regulatory regime (arts 12 and 22).

(b) An insurer's assets had to exceed its liabilities for its entire business by a margin to be calculated under the Directive (the 'solvency margin', as set out in art 16). The assets which could be taken into account were defined. Where an insurer failed to

5. Council Directive 73/240 of 24 July 1973 abolishing restrictions on freedom of establishment in the business of direct insurance other than life assurance.

meet its solvency margin, each member state was required to lay down remedial measures, in the form of the proposal by the insurer of a short term plan to restore its fortunes, coupled with the availability of administrative powers to prevent the insurer from issuing new policies (art 20). Ultimately, this could lead to administrative winding up.

(c) An insurer with its head office within the EC was entitled to establish a branch or agency in any other member state by seeking authorisation from, and submitting a scheme of operations to, the host authority. However, certification by the insurer's home state authorities that it had satisfied the solvency margin was to be conclusive evidence of that fact in the host state (arts 10 and 11).

(d) An insurer was required to maintain sufficient technical reserves in each member state in which it was authorised, those reserves to be in the form of assets realisable in local currency (art 15).

(e) Insurers with their head offices outside the EC were to be free to establish agencies or branches within the EC, but subject to stricter authorisation requirements (art 23).

The First Non-Life Directive was subsequently extended to cover tourist assistance (thereby resolving a previous debate as to whether such protection was insurance at all, by bringing tourist assistance within the regulatory regime but excluding ordinary domestic motor breakdown cover) and credit and suretyship insurance, creating eighteen classes of non-life business.[6]

Nevertheless, much was left to domestic law. In particular, those countries which had previously maintained material control in respect of policy terms and premium levels remained entitled to do so, over both their own insurers and the establishments of insurers with head offices in other member states.

---

[6] Respectively: Council Directive 84/641 of 10 December 1984 amending, particularly as regards tourist assistance, the First Directive on the co-ordination of laws, regulations and administrative provisions relating to the taking-up and pursuit of the business of direct insurance other than life assurance; Council Directive 87/343 of 22 June 1987 amending, as regards credit insurance and suretyship insurance, the First Directive on the co-ordination of laws, regulations and administrative provisions relating to the taking-up and pursuit of the business of direct insurance other than life assurance. The Directives do not at present extend to export credit insurance, although a proposal for such an extension was introduced by the Commission in 1995.

*Life insurance*

Equivalent measures for life insurance were not adopted until 1979. The First Life Directive[7] more or less echoed the principles set out in the First Non-Life Directive as regards prior authorisation on a class by class basis for the nine classes of life insurance business and freedom of establishment. The First Life Directive, adopting the position which had prevailed in the majority of member states prior to its implementation, placed a prohibition on the creation of new *composite* insurers, i.e., insurers carrying on both life and non-life business (art 8). Composites which had been established were permitted to continue as such, but subject to a strict separation of business which involved keeping non-life and life funds separate and which imposed upon life offices particularly strenuous accounting obligations (art 8). The reason for this policy was that, historically, life insurance has proved to be far more profitable than non-life insurance, the former being less susceptible to sudden variations in the incidence of loss, and it was felt to be necessary to prevent profits from the life insurance account being used to subsidise general insurance business.

## The 'Second Generation' Insurance Directives

### Co-insurance and the insurance cases

Having set up the principle of freedom of establishment, the next step for the Commission was to introduce free movement of insurance services within the EC, by allowing an insurer authorised and established in any member state to sell insurance in any other member state without the need for further authorisation or establishment. The Commission's ambitions were, however, thwarted by a series of cases, collectively known as the insurance cases, which were brought by the Commission against various member states for their failure to implement the Co-Insurance Directive of 1978.[8] This Directive was a modest provision laying down the first steps toward free movement of insurance services

---

7. Council Directive 79/267 of 5 March 1979 on the co-ordination of laws, regulations and administrative provisions relating to the taking-up and pursuit of the business of direct life assurance.
8. Council Directive 78/473 of 30 May 1978 on the co-ordination of laws, regulations and administrative provisions relating to Community co-insurance.

and applied to the insurance of major risks by a number of insurers from different countries. Such arrangements are very common, and in practice operate by means of the appointment of a leading insurer who has delegated to him responsibility for administering the contract and, in some circumstances, reaching a settlement with the assured. The Co-Insurance Directive required member states to lift restrictions on the participation in co-insurance within the EC by EC-based insurers. In particular a participating co-insurer was not required to seek authorisation in the state in which the leading insurer had its head office, and issues of technical reserves were left to the authorities of the member state in which each participating co-insurer was established (arts 2 to 4).

In the insurance cases, Case 252/83 *Commission v Denmark*,[9] Case 205/84 *Commission v Germany*,[10] Case 206/84 *Commission v Ireland*[11] and Case 220/83 *Commission v France*,[12] the Commission in enforcement proceedings brought before the European Court of Justice challenged various domestic rules, namely:

(a) as regards a risk located within a member state, the requirement that the leading insurer had to be authorised and established in that member state;

(b) brokers within a member state could arrange risks located in that state only with insurers authorised and established in that state;

(c) co-insurance was permissible only where the sum insured exceeded a particular minimum figure;

(d) an insurer with its head office in a member state was required to obtain authorisation from the regulatory authorities of that state in order to provide insurance in any other member state.

Points (c) and (d) gave rise to little difficulty. The Court ruled as to (c) that there was no objection to the imposition of thresholds,[13] and as to (d) that this restriction was not discriminatory or unduly restrictive. The key questions were raised by points (a) and (b), as

---

[9.] [1986] ECR 3713, [1987] 2 CMLR 169.   [10.] [1986] ECR 3755, [1987] 2 CMLR 69.   [11.] [1986] ECR 3817, [1987] 2 CMLR 150.   [12.] [1986] ECR 3663, [1987] 2 CMLR 113.

[13.] The Co-Insurance Directive was subsequently amended by the Second Non-Life Directive 1988 to restrict its operation to 'large risks', i.e., substantial commercial risks: see pp 10 and 147–8 for the meaning of this concept.

these raised squarely the scope of freedom permitted to an insurer authorised and established in one member state to insure risks located within another member state. The Court's ruling was only partially helpful to the Commission's plans. The Court ruled that where an insurer was authorised and established in member state A but wished to sell insurance in member state B, then: (i) if the insurer set up a branch or agency in member state B, that branch or agency could be required to comply with member state B's rules on authorisation and supervision; (ii) if the insurer wished to sell insurance in member state B other than through a branch or agency established in member state B, the regulatory authorities of member state B could not insist upon the insurer setting up a branch or agency, it being sufficient for the insurer to have some form of permanent representation; (iii) the authorities of member state B could impose upon the insurer the requirement of authorisation in so far as this was necessary in the wider public interest to protect consumers in the interests of the 'general good'.

The final part of this ruling meant that the Commission could not move directly to a structure whereby authorisation in member state A provided a licence to sell in member state B without the need to seek authorisation in member state B. Instead, the Commission developed a compromise position whereby an insurer established and authorised in member state A could sell insurance directly into member state B without authorisation, provided that the persons being insured were not in need of the protection conferred by authorisation. A different technique was adopted for each of the broad categories of non-life and life insurance.

### Non-life insurance

The Second Non-Life Directive of 1988[14] extended the right of establishment by providing, in line with the insurance cases, that an insurer could operate in another member state through a permanent presence rather than a fully fledged branch or agency. The Directive also extended the First Non-Life Directive into the field of compulsory insurance. Its main impact, however, was to take the first steps towards free movement of insurance services for

---

14. Council Directive 88/357 of 22 June 1988 on the co-ordination of laws, regulations and administrative provisions relating to direct insurance other than life insurance and laying down provisions to facilitate the effective exercise of freedom to provide services.

most forms of insurance: at this stage compulsory insurances, particularly road traffic and employers' liability, were excluded, although these were subsequently incorporated into the regulatory structure in 1990.[15] An insurer established and authorised in member state A was empowered to sell insurance directly to policyholders in member state B, without any establishment in member state B.

At this point a distinction was drawn between 'large risks' and 'mass risks' (a distinction which is also relevant for choice of law purposes – see chapter 6). Large risks were risks of a commercial nature, including transport insurance and credit insurance irrespective of the identity of the assured, and property and liability risks where the assured met minimum turnover requirements or minimum numbers of employees: a risk of the latter type was a large risk if the assured satisfied any two of three criteria – balance sheet turnover of 12.4 million ECU, net turnover of 24 million ECU, and 500 average number of persons employed. These figures prevailed for the transitional period between 30 June 1990 (the Directive's due date of implementation) and 31 December 1992; thereafter, the relevant figures were balance sheet turnover of 6.2 million ECU, net turnover of 12.8 million ECU, and 250 average number of persons employed. In the case of large risks, the insurer was free to sell into member state B provided only that the insurer at the outset informed the regulatory authorities of member state B of its intentions and of the nature of the risks to be covered.

By contrast, in the case of 'mass risks', i.e., insurances of a consumer nature, member states remained free to impose an authorisation requirement, involving the submission of a scheme of operations, on an insurer wishing to sell insurance into its territory by means of services, that is, without any establishment in the host state. This distinction reflected the Court's ruling in the insurance cases that member states should be free to regulate insurers on consumer protection and 'general good' grounds. The Directive also contained a series of protective measures for assureds who wished to take advantage of the opportunity to obtain insurance from an insurer operating elsewhere in the EC:

---

15. By Council Directive 90/618 of 8 November 1990. Special provision was necessary given the need to harmonise the substantive law on this matter: see chapter 3.

(a) member states remained free to impose material control over policy terms and premium levels, providing that such rules did not go beyond what was necessary to achieve their aims (art 19);

(b) common rules were laid down for choice of law for insurance contracts, the general idea being that an assured should receive the protection of the law of his home state even though the insurer was located outside that state, subject to the right of the parties to contract out of this position if the assured's domestic law so allowed (art 7);[16]

(c) an assured intending to obtain insurance from an insurer authorised and established elsewhere in the EC had to be given pre-contract warnings in standard form informing him that the insurer was from another member state (art 21);

(d) insurers offering insurance by way of services could be required to contribute to policyholder protection schemes operated by the host state, providing fall-back cover against insurers becoming insolvent (art 24).

*Life insurance*

The Second Life Directive of 1990[17] brought life insurance into line with non-life insurance. The most important point of contrast derives from the fact that it was necessary to devise some method of distinguishing between assureds who needed protection and those who did not: plainly, the 'large risks' and 'mass risks' distinction relevant for non-life purposes was inappropriate to life insurance. The solution adopted was for a distinction to be drawn between ordinary policyholders, and policyholders who had 'taken the initiative in seeking the commitment'. A policyholder fell into the latter class in two situations: (i) where the policy was not solicited by the insurer by means of advertising or any form of approach to the policyholder by the insurer or his agent, and the contract was made either in the insurer's home state or by each of the parties in their own home states; or (ii) where the policyholder himself approached an intermediary with a view to procuring a

16. For choice of law generally, see chapter 6.
17. Council Directive 90/619 of 8 November 1990 on the co-ordination of laws, regulations and administrative provisions relating to direct life assurance, laying down provisions to facilitate the effective exercise of freedom to provide services.

policy underwritten by an insurer located in another member state, and had signed a standard form statement to that effect. If either of these situations applied, so that the policyholder had taken the initiative in seeking the commitment, the policyholder was thought not to be in need of protection and the insurer was free to sell the policy to the assured without seeking authorisation from the assured's home state regulatory authorities, provided that they were informed of the insurer's activities at the outset. By contrast, where the policyholder had not taken the initiative in dealing with an insurer authorised and established elsewhere in the EC, the insurer was required to be authorised by the regulatory authorities of the assured's home state, which again entailed submitting to the authorities a scheme of operations for the insurer's activities in that territory (see generally, Title III of the Directive).

As with the Second Non-Life Directive, consumer protection measures were laid down in the Second Life Directive:

(a) choice of law rules were laid down, providing the initial presumption that the assured was to retain the benefit of the application of his domestic law to the policy, subject to contracting out provisions where domestic law so permitted (art 4);
(b) the policyholder was required to sign a statement in standard form recognising that the insurer was located in another member state;
(c) the Directive required member states to introduce a cooling-off period of between fourteen and thirty days, in which period the policyholder had the right to cancel the policy (art 15);
(d) material controls over terms and premium rates could be maintained.

## The 'Third Generation' Insurance Directives

The Third Generation of Insurance Directives completed[18] the slow progress towards the Single European Insurance Market, by abolishing for all but fall-back purposes the right of a host state to insist upon authorising the activities of an insurer established and authorised in some other member state, whether the insurer's

---

18. Subject to one minor modification, introduced by Council Directive 95/26, concerning supervisory powers.

activities in the host state are conducted through a branch, agency or establishment located in the host state, or whether they are conducted by means of direct selling from an establishment located elsewhere in the EC. The Third Non-Life and Third Life Directives[19] are more or less the same in format, and have the following features.

(a) An insurer with its head office in a member state must seek authorisation from the regulatory authorities of that state. Authorisation is on a class by class basis, with a prohibition on new authorisations of composite life and non-life insurers, and on the carrying on of any other form of business by an insurer along with its insurance business. Controllers and substantial shareholders (encompassing persons whose holdings reach or increase to 20%, 33% or 50%) must be fit and proper persons, and authorisation and the maintenance of authorisation are dependent upon the insurer satisfying its home authorities that it will operate and is operating on the basis of 'sound and prudent' management. The Directives also place controls on the transfer of insurance undertakings.

(b) Member states are no longer permitted to impose material controls on policy terms and premium levels.

(c) Authorisation operates as a Single European Licence, allowing an authorised insurer without authorisation from any other member state (i) to establish a branch or agency elsewhere in the EC (right of establishment) and (ii) to sell insurance into any member state from an establishment in any other member state (provision of insurance by way of services). For the purposes of provision of insurance by way of services, the distinction drawn in the Second Generation Directives between large and mass risks, and between policyholders who sought the commitment and those who did not, is abolished. An insurer who wishes to exercise the right to sell insurance outside its own territory can do so merely by informing the regulatory authorities of the host of its intention to do so, and by obtaining supporting documentation from its home authorities.

19. Respectively: Third Council Directive 92/49 of 18 June 1992 on the co-ordination of laws, regulations and administrative provisions relating to direct insurance other than life assurance; and Third Council Directive 92/96 of 10 December 1992 on the co-ordination of laws, regulations and administrative provisions relating to direct life assurance.

(d) Technical provisions must be adequate in respect of the entirety of the insurer's business, but assets need not be localised in any one member state – it is enough that they are held within the EC.

(e) Post-authorisation regulation is to be carried out by the regulatory authorities of the insurer's home state, and in particular the insurer must adhere to solvency margin requirements or face remedial action by its home authorities. Home state authorities are given wide powers to regulate the EC-wide activities of their insurers, including withdrawal of authorisation and the preservation of assets.

(f) Mergers between insurers and transfers of insurance business are regulated on an EC-wide basis, the general rule being that an insurer authorised in one member state and in a state of solvency is normally to be permitted to procure the business of another insurer located in another territory, subject to the approval of the authorities of the member state in which the transferor is authorised and of the authorities of the member state in which the business has been transacted.

(g) Member states retain limited residual powers to protect their policyholders, in two respects. First, where the regulatory authorities of the insurer's home state fail to act to prevent the insurer from infringing the host's domestic law, the host's regulatory authorities may step in and take action, but only as a last resort. Secondly, member states may impose restrictions on contracts in 'the general good'. This concept is not specific to insurance, and refers to any legislation which is of a consumer protection nature. There were fears that member states might, intentionally or otherwise, operate a form of national protectionism by imposing general good measures with which insurers from other member states are unable to comply while at the same time maintaining cost-effectiveness. One illustration is the requirement in some member states that consumer contracts are in the consumer's language. The experience to date has been that such measures have not been used to stifle competition, but this does not mean that they do not constitute a serious barrier to competition.

(h) Choice of law rules apply to risks located within the EC: these are discussed in detail in chapter 6.

The Single Insurance Market came into existence on 1 July

1994, the implementation date of the Third Generation of Directives. Transitional arrangements for Spain operate until the end of 1996 and for Greece and Portugal operate until the end of 1998. The operation of the Single Insurance Market is kept under review by the Insurance Committee, established by Council Regulation in 1991 and commencing its work on 1 January 1992.[20] The Committee's main role is to propose to the Commission amendments to the Directives in the light of experience and developments in the insurance market.

## The European Economic Area

The formation of the European Economic Area (EEA) as between the countries of the EC and EFTA (excluding Switzerland), with effect from 1 January 1994 has had the effect of expanding the single insurance market. Under the EEA agreement, EFTA countries participate in the insurance market on the basis of the three Generations of Insurance Directives. Special arrangements have also been made for Switzerland, under provisions of the First and Second Generation Directives which allow reciprocal agreements between the EC and non-member countries. The broad effect of the agreement between the EC and Switzerland is to extend to Switzerland access to the EC's non-life insurance market on the basis of the Second Non-Life Directive, with reciprocal access being granted by EC insurers to the Swiss non-life market.[21]

## Other legislation

### Accounting provisions

From an early stage in the development of the general Single Market the EC saw the need to develop standard accounting rules for companies operating within the EC, thereby allowing investors and creditors to compare like with like across member states.

---

20. Council Regulation 675/91 of 19 December 1991 setting up an insurance committee.
21. The agreement takes effect as Council Regulation 2155/91 of 20 June 1991 and Council Decision 91/370 of 20 June 1991. Member states were required to implement the Regulation and Decision by Council Directive 91/371 on the implementation of the Agreement between the European Economic Community and the Swiss Confederation concerning direct insurance other than life assurance.

There has been a series of Directives on company accounts, the most important being the Fourth Directive adopted in 1978, which sets out the form which corporate annual accounts – the balance sheet, the profit and loss account and accompanying notes – must take, and the Seventh Directive, which is concerned with the presentation of consolidated accounts for corporate groups.[22] In the first instance neither Directive applied to the accounts of insurance companies (or, for that matter, banks), on the basis that more elaborate provisions were required given the special nature of insurance business. An insurance accounting Directive was finally adopted in 1991,[23] which is based on the rules applicable to companies in general but modified by requiring greater disclosure of forms of investment.

### The Legal Expenses Insurance Directive

The Legal Expenses Insurance Directive of 1987[24] is essentially a consumer protection measure, aimed at eliminating any possible conflict of interest which might face an insurer who is liable to pay the legal costs of a party to legal proceedings. One example might be the situation in which A has caused injury to B and the liability insurer of A is also the legal expenses insurer of B: it is readily conceivable that pressure might be put on B, by refusal of his legal expenses claim, not to pursue A. The Directive thus adopts a strict separation of the provision of legal expenses insurance from the provision of other forms of insurance by the same insurer, which may be done either by: (i) the erection of a 'Chinese Wall' within the insurer's organisation, so that no person deals with both legal expenses insurance and any other class of business; or (ii) the separation of legal expenses insurance into a subsidiary; or (iii) the conferring on the assured of the contractual right to instruct his own lawyer.[25]

---

22. Respectively: Council Directive 78/660 of 25 July 1978 on the annual accounts of certain types of companies; and Council Directive 83/349 of 13 June 1983 on consolidated accounts.

23. Council Directive 91/674 of 19 December 1991 on the annual accounts and consolidated accounts of insurance undertakings.

24. Council Directive 87/344 of 22 June 1987 on the co-ordination of laws, regulations and administrative provisions relating to legal expenses insurance.

25. The Directive allows member states to choose one of these possibilities, or to leave it to insurers to choose which of the three approaches to adopt. The UK, consistently with its liberal approach to insurance matters, has, in its implementation of the Directive, left the choice to insurers: Legal Expenses Insurance Regulations 1990, SI 1990 No 1159.

*Winding up*

The harmonisation of the regulation of insurance companies has to date stopped short of determining the circumstances in which an insurance company can be wound up and the consequences of winding up for the insurer's assets. The Commission has in the past regarded this as a vital issue for the single insurance market, but to date it has been unsuccessful in pursuing its ideas into legislation: one of the main stumbling blocks appears to have been the fact that insolvency law varies considerably as between the member states, and any attempt to harmonise even this aspect of winding up necessarily has far wider implications. The Commission first put forward a proposal for a Directive on the compulsory winding up of insurance companies in March 1987, and an amended proposal was published in September 1989, but the Council has yet to give its approval.[26]

The proposed Directive would provide for the automatic winding up of an insurer whose authorisation was withdrawn following its failure to maintain adherence to the criteria for authorisation as laid down by the Insurance Directives. Two forms of winding up are contemplated. *Normal compulsory winding up* is to be carried out by the insurer itself, although there can be supervisory authority intervention where the winding up is not progressing satisfactorily. The effect of winding up, which is to take effect throughout the EC, is to leave existing policies operative, but to prevent their renewal. The regulatory authorities of the state in which the insurer has its head office are to be charged with the duty of ensuring that the insurer either tries to transfer its portfolio of policies or terminates them in accordance with their terms. *Special compulsory winding up* is to be ordered by the regulatory authorities, generally on the ground of insolvency, and is to be carried out by liquidators appointed by them for the purpose. Non-life policies are to terminate automatically after 30 days, whereas life policies are to remain effective. Again, the ultimate object is to secure the transfer of the insurer's portfolio to another, suitable, insurer.

---

26. See OJ 1987 C71/5 and OJ 1989 C252/5 for the two versions of the proposed Directive.

# The operation of the single market: the UK experience

## Outline of UK legislation

The operation of the Single Insurance Market is best illustrated by an outline of the UK's implementation of the EC's Directives. The relevant legislation is the Insurance Companies Act 1982, which has been amended by statutory instrument on over twenty occasions in order to take account of the developing single market for insurance. Supplementary legislation relevant to the implementation of EC law, of which the reader should be aware consists of:

- the Financial Services Act 1986, which lays down a distinct regulatory regime for investment contracts, including most forms of life insurance – the Act has been amended to comply with EC requirements;
- the Friendly Societies Act 1992, which regulates the forms of (mainly) life insurance offered by friendly societies – the legislation extends the Insurance Companies Act 1982 to those societies ('directive friendly societies') which offer insurance outside the UK;
- the Companies Act 1985, as amended, which contains the accounting provisions for insurance companies;
- the Insurance Companies Regulations 1994, SI 1994 No 1516, which supplement the 1982 Act;
- the Insurance Companies (Accounts and Statements) Regulations 1996, SI 1996 No 943, which set out the form of various documents to be maintained by insurers – the Regulations replace SI 1983 No 1811, and, in accordance with government policy on 'red tape', are rather less daunting than their predecessors;
- the Insurance Companies (Legal Expenses) Insurance Regulations 1990, SI 1990 No 1159, which implement the Legal Expenses Insurance Directive.

The UK system has, where an option has been given, for the most part operated in a fashion more liberal than that actually required by the Insurance Directives. From an early stage the Insurance Companies Act 1982 permitted insurers authorised and established in other member states to become established in the

UK and to sell insurance into the UK without UK authorisation: in particular the consumer protection measures introduced by the Second Generation Directives, based on the distinction between large and mass risks and assureds who sought the commitment, were thought not to be necessary, and almost complete freedom was granted to EC insurers wishing to operate in the UK on the implementation of those Directives. Moreover, the UK has not expressly reserved to itself the power to protect consumer assureds on the basis of the 'general good' as permitted by the Third Generation Directives, and there are remarkably few pieces of UK legislation which are likely to affect insurance contracts. Perhaps the only example is the Unfair Terms in Consumer Contracts Regulations 1994 (see chapter 2), but these Regulations merely implement the EC's Unfair Terms in Consumer Contracts Directive of 1993, so that the law on unfair terms in consumer contracts is more or less the same in all member states.

The UK experience has nevertheless thrown up a number of problems which have as yet not been resolved on an EC-wide basis.

## Authorisation under UK law

### UK business

In accordance with the freedoms created by the Directives, the Insurance Companies Act 1982 sets out rules for the authorisation of various forms of insurance activity.[27] The basic principle is that an insurer who wishes to carry on insurance business in the UK is required to obtain authorisation on a class by class basis from the Insurance Division of the Department of Trade and Industry (DTI). The law prohibits a new applicant from being authorised for both life and non-life insurance. UK authorisation is not, however, required of an insurer with its head office in another EC or EFTA member state, or a Swiss non-life insurer, and which is authorised to carry on insurance business by its home authorities. Such an insurer is free to establish a branch or agency in the UK, or sell directly into the UK, subject only to notifying the DTI when it first intends to do so and arranging for certification of its

---

27. The details are contained in the Insurance Companies Act 1982, ss 1 to 14 and Scheds 2E to 2G.

solvency and of the scope of its authorisation to be provided by its home state regulatory authorities.

Authorisation is, therefore, required only of UK insurers and insurers located outside the EEA. To obtain authorisation, the insurer must submit a scheme of operations setting out the nature of its business and financial projections, and must demonstrate that its controllers are fit and proper persons who will ensure that the insurer's business is managed on 'sound and prudent' lines: the sound and prudent management condition is an EC concept, and is defined by the 1982 Act as including skill and integrity, appropriate levels of accounting and adherence to domestic law.[28] It should also be stressed that the regulated activity is 'carrying on insurance business in the UK', a concept defined by s 95 of the 1982 Act as consisting of the effecting and carrying out of insurance contracts and held by the House of Lords in *Scher and Ackman v Policyholders Protection Board*[29] to refer to the overall conduct of the insurer's business and not merely to isolated aspects of it. An insurer based in the UK which is making underwriting decisions in the UK is, therefore, as demonstrated by *Scher* itself, carrying on business in the UK even though its policyholders are based abroad and claims are paid abroad in foreign currencies, whereas an insurer represented in the UK by an agent who does not have authority to make binding underwriting decisions or to settle on behalf of the insurer may not be carrying on insurance business in the UK and thus may not require UK authorisation.[30] Where an insurer is not authorised to carry on insurance business in the UK, but nevertheless does so, it commits a criminal offence but any policies issued by it are enforceable at the instance of the assured and the insurer is not precluded by its illegality from seeking indemnification from its reinsurers.[31]

28. Insurance Companies Act 1982, Sched 2A.     29. [1993] 3 All ER 408.
30. It was decided by the Court of Appeal in *Re Great Western Insurance* 1996, unreported, that whether or not an insurer carries on insurance business through an agent depends upon the agent's authority, and that the absence of any power to make contracts is only one indication. The Court of Appeal reversed the ruling of Parker J in *Re Companies 007116 and 007118 to 007124 of 1994*, 1995, unreported, a decision which concentrated solely on the power of the agent to make contracts, and accordingly which made evasion of the regulatory structure – by the use of offshore insurers in 'havens' and having the ultimate (if only nominal) power to accept or reject risks – comparatively simple. Soliciting business is also carrying on insurance business: *R v Wilson* 1996, unreported. For the position of the agent in the regulatory structure, see chapter 4, below.
31. Financial Services Act 1986, s 132, reversing the Court of Appeal's ruling in *Phoenix General Insurance Co of Greece SA v ADAS* [1988] QB 216 that a

*EEA business*

Under the scheme of the Single European Licence, the UK authorities are responsible for providing authorisation to UK based insurers to carry on insurance business or to sell insurance by way of services not just in the UK but throughout the EEA. A UK authorisation granted to a UK company is, therefore, effective to provide authorisation to the insurer to carry on insurance business in any other member state. To obtain the Single European Licence, the insurer must notify to the DTI the member states in which it intends to set up an establishment and the nature of the business to be conducted by the establishment, and the DTI must then forward the relevant information to the host state authorities together with certification of the insurer's solvency and authorisation. A similar regime, but less onerous in terms of the provision of information, operates where a UK insurer wishes to sell insurance elsewhere in the EC by way of services rather than by means of the creation of an establishment. Once these minimal requirements are satisfied, a UK insurer is free to trade elsewhere in the EC. Any infringement of these requirements constitutes a criminal offence in the UK under s 71 of the 1982 Act.

While there is a clear distinction drawn, at least for the purposes of home state authorisation and regulation, between carrying on insurance business in another member state through an establishment, branch or agency, and selling insurance direct by way of services, the insurance market itself does not operate in quite such a clear cut fashion. At the extremes of operating through a subsidiary or by means of direct telephone marketing, there is no real difficulty of classification. More problematic is the typical arrangement operated by English insurers whereby a local agent is appointed and is given a binding authority to accept risks up to a certain level. If the present case law referred to above is correct, then as a matter of English law the use of 'binders' in another member state means that the insurer is carrying on insurance business in that state and must comply with the establishment rather than the services rules, and the DTI generally

---

31. *(continued)* policy made by an unauthorised insurer is illegal and that the insurer's reinsurances are thereby invalidated. Section 132 has been held by the Court of Appeal to be retroactive, and validates all claims made after the section came into force whenever the policy was made: *Group Josi Re v Walbrook Insurance* [1996] 1 All ER 791; the House of Lords subsequently refused leave to appeal.

so insists. It is far from clear, however, that this is the position under EC law. The European Commission is known to have considered the problem but has yet to issue any guidance: unofficially, the Commission's view is that every case has to be looked at on its facts.

## Post-authorisation supervision

### Regulation of UK-authorised insurers

The controls over UK-authorised insurers by the DTI, contained in ss 15 to 71 of the Insurance Companies Act 1982 are detailed and complex. The key point here is that these controls apply to the entirety of an insurer's EEA business, and not just to the UK aspects of those businesses, and as a corollary the UK authorities have almost exclusive jurisdiction to exercise remedial powers where an insurer infringes the domestic requirements of any other member state by its dealings in that state. The right of any host state to interfere with the operations of a UK-based insurer is limited to providing assistance to the UK authorities, normally by way of seeking information from the insurer (which may be done by a host state on its own initiative in the case of a branch or agency) or by freezing its assets following a request by the DTI. The one major exception to the non-intervention principle concerns the right of member states under the Third Generation of Directives to restrict freedom of contract 'in the general good'. This right, which acts as a substitute for the right to seek authorisation in consumer cases conferred by the Second Generation of Directives but removed by the Third Generation, allows member states to maintain consumer protection and related measures. However, material controls over policy terms and premium levels cannot be exercised as a result of the Third Generation of Directives.

The controls which may be exercised over UK-authorised insurers by the DTI reflect the EC's regulatory harmonisation programme: the one respect in which UK law goes further than the Directives is in the context of winding up which, as noted above, has yet to be harmonised. The controls established by the 1982 Act can be summarised as follows. The regulatory position is necessarily more or less the same in each member state as regards insurers established and authorised in that state.

First, an insurer is not permitted, under s 16 of the 1982 Act, to carry on insurance business with any form of business not connected with insurance business, the object being to preserve the insurance fund and to prevent it being used to finance other, perhaps more speculative, ventures. This section has given rise to a good deal of difficulty, as there is no guidance on exactly when business is connected to insurance business, but on a day to day level the point is largely immaterial as there are no criminal sanctions against an insurer who does carry on other forms of business, and the validity of the contracts themselves is unaffected.[32]

Secondly, there are harmonised rules for the preparation of accounts and statements, implementing the EC corporate accounting and group accounting Directives.[33] Special rules are laid down for life insurance, in particular the requirement for an annual actuarial investigation of this form of business.

Thirdly, as demanded by the Directives, there is a strict separation of the assets and liabilities attributable to life business and assets and liabilities attributable to non-life business,[34] to prevent cross-subsidisation of non-life losses by life profits. Separate accounting is required, and transfers from the life fund are permissible only where the life fund is in surplus and a distribution has been made to policyholders.

Fourthly, and perhaps the key feature of the harmonised regime, is the requirement for a UK insurer to maintain a solvency margin for both UK and EC,[35] coupled with a minimum guarantee fund which forms part of the solvency margin. Assets and liabilities which may or must be taken into account are carefully defined, and there is a procedure whereby an insurer whose assets do not exceed liabilities by the required margin is to be required to remedy the deficiency by the preparation of a plan to restore solvency. If the minimum guarantee fund is not maintained a short-term financial scheme must be agreed with the DTI. The Act also imposes requirements on the maintenance of assets and on the currencies in which assets are to be realisable, in order to comply

---

32. So held by the Court of Appeal in *Fuji Finance Inc v Aetna Life Insurance Co Ltd* [1996] 4 All ER 608.

33. Insurance Companies Act 1982, ss 17 to 27: the form of accounts is provided for by SI 1996 No 943 and the Companies Act 1985, ss 255 and 255A.

34. Insurance Companies Act 1982, ss 28 to 31.

35. Insurance Companies Act 1982, ss 32 to 35B. The detail is contained in SI 1994 No 1516.

with the localisation and matching rules in the First Generation of Directives.

Fifthly, ss 37 to 59 of the 1982 Act set out the powers which may be exercised against an insurer which has failed to comply with the various regulatory measures laid down in the Act. The grounds on which powers may be exercised include: the insurer's potential insolvency, including inadequate reinsurance arrangements; failure by the insurer to conduct its business in accordance with the criteria of sound and prudent management; failure by the insurer to adhere to the requirements of regulatory legislation; and the provision of false or misleading accounting or other information. The powers themselves include: regulating the insurer's future investments; requiring the insurer to maintain assets in the UK, possibly by means of transfer to the custody of a trustee; restricting the insurer's ability to dispose of certain assets; limiting the premium income which the insurer may receive; instigating investigations and demanding information, backed with the ability to search premises; and, ultimately, the presentation of a winding up petition to the court in respect of the insurer. It has already been observed that the grounds for and the consequences of the winding up of insurance companies have yet to be harmonised on an EC-wide basis. The UK rules on the matter at present provide that winding up petitions may be presented in the usual way, most importantly by unsatisfied creditors, but with a number of differences: the Secretary of State may himself seek a winding up order; a life insurer may not be wound up other than in compulsory liquidation proceedings; the court has a discretion to reduce the insurance liabilities of an insolvent insurer as an alternative to winding up; and in the case of life business the liquidator must carry on the business with a view to arranging its transfer to another insurer.[36] The practice in the UK is for an insolvent insurer to be put into provisional liquidation so that its business can, wherever possible, be preserved.

---

36. Insurance Companies Act 1982, ss 53 to 59. English law also makes provision for the protection of policyholders of insolvent insurers. If there is no claim against the insurer when it is wound up, the policyholder is entitled to prove in the insurer's liquidation for value of the unexpired part of the premium, calculated in accordance with the Insurance Companies (Winding Up) Rules 1985, SI 1985 No 95. If there is a claim against the insurer at this date, a private policyholder under a UK policy is entitled to claim at least 90% (and in the case of compulsory insurance, 100%) of the loss from the Policyholders Protection Board: Policyholders Protection Act 1975.

Sixthly, the 1982 Act confers, in accordance with the Third Generation Directives, strict controls over the persons participating in an insurer's affairs. An insurer who employs a person unfit to hold a particular office can be made the subject of the regulatory powers outlined in the previous paragraph,[37] the DTI must approve the appointment of the managing director or chief executive of an insurance company and any new controller of the company, and acquisitions of 'notifiable' shareholdings – 25%, 33% and 50% – are equally subject to prior approval.[38]

Finally, the 1982 Act implements the insurance Directives' rules on the transfers of insurance business as between insurers in different member states.[39] These are based on the single market principles which underlie the entire regulatory structure. In outline, the transfer of EC life insurance business carried on by a UK insurer requires judicial approval, and the transfer of EC non-life insurance business carried on by a UK insurer requires DTI approval. In each case the transferee's regulatory authorities must have certified that the transferee is both authorised and in possession of the necessary margin of solvency, and the member state in which the business is located must also approve of the transfer. Where business transacted in the UK is transferred between insurers in other member states, the UK has in the legislation waived its right to withhold its consent to the transfer. A transfer, when approved, binds policyholders.

*Regulation of EC and EFTA insurers*

Where the insurer is one established and authorised in another member state then, in accordance with the concept of the Single European Licence, the DTI's supervisory powers over it are minimal and residual. The regulatory provisions, which vary in detail as between EC and EFTA insurers, applicable to insurers from within the EEA are the following:[40]

(a) where the insurer has failed to maintain its solvency margin, the DTI may prevent the disposal of its assets after a request so to act by the insurer's home regulatory authorities;

37. Insurance Companies Act 1982, s 46.
38. Insurance Companies Act 1982, ss 60 to 64 and Sched 2D.
39. Insurance Companies Act 1982, ss 49 to 52B and Sched 2C.
40. Insurance Companies Act 1982, Sched 2F.

(b) the DTI may obtain information from the insurer at the request of its home regulatory authorities in order to allow those authorities to carry out their regulatory functions, and an insurer which is carrying on insurance business in the UK is required to maintain proper accounting records in respect of that business in the UK;[41]

(c) where the insurer has failed to comply with UK law after a request to do so, the DTI may request the insurer's home authorities to act, although in urgent cases the DTI may demand compliance without reference to the insurer's own regulatory authorities;

(d) where the insurer's authorisation has been withdrawn by its own regulatory authorities, the DTI may order the insurer to cease carrying on insurance business in the UK, without prejudice to the performance of existing contracts.

It has already been noted that the Third Generation Insurance Directives authorise member states to impose restrictions on freedom of contract 'in the general good'. This option has not been taken up in the UK, with the result that EC insurers are largely free from DTI interference unless there has been a request to the DTI for assistance from the insurer's home regulatory authorities. The closest that the UK has come to legislating to protect the general good specifically in the insurance context is the residual power set out in (c) above to intervene in an 'urgent' case where for some reason the assistance of the insurer's home authorities cannot be called upon to assist.

### Regulation of the conduct of UK insurance business

Sections 72 to 81 of the Insurance Companies Act 1982 regulate insurance business carried on in the UK irrespective of the nationality of the insurer. The statutory rules for the most part implement requirements of the Insurance Directives, but there are some provisions which are unique to the UK and which do not touch upon the harmonisation programme. In outline:

(a) insurance advertisements which specify the insurer's share capital must indicate how much of that capital is subscribed and paid up;[42]

---

41. Insurance Companies Act 1982, s 27.
42. Insurance Companies Act 1982, s 72 and SI 1994 No 1516.

(b) policyholders are entitled to be given information – prior to the conclusion of the contract the policyholder must be given details of the cover (life insurance) or complaints procedures (non-life insurance) and of the address of the insurer's establishment issuing the contract, and after the conclusion of the contract the policyholder must be given details of any changes in the information provided (life insurance);[43]

(c) intermediaries must inform potential assureds of their own connection with the insurer, and whether the insurer is authorised outside the EEA;[44]

(d) a cooling-off period is laid down for life insurance, the right of cancellation being exercisable by the policyholder within ten days running from the date on which the policyholder is given a statutory notice of the right to cancel.[45]

43. Insurance Companies Act 1982, ss 72A, 72B and Sched 2E.
44. Insurance Companies Act 1982, s 74 and SI 1994 No 1516.
45. Insurance Companies Act 1982, ss 75 to 77.

# CHAPTER TWO

# Insurance contracts

## Insurance contracts in domestic law

### The general picture

The law of insurance contracts in England is derived almost exclusively from the common law dating back to the middle of the eighteenth century, and remains today essentially a set of judge-made rules. There was an attempt, in the Marine Insurance Act 1906, to codify without intentional modification the principles applicable to marine insurance, but there is no equivalent code relating to the non-marine market and even the 1906 Act itself can no longer be regarded as comprehensive given the changes in market practice and standard-form documentation since it was passed. Legislation is almost exclusively regulatory, and much of the legislation was adopted to implement EC Directives.[1] There have been various statutory interventions which affect the contract itself, but these are relatively minor in their impact on ordinary contracts. Perhaps the most important pieces of legislation are: the Life Assurance Act 1774 (prohibition on the use of life policies in the form of wagering on lives); the Third Parties (Rights against Insurers) Act 1930 (which, in the case of liability insurance, transfers the insurance claim of an insolvent assured to the victim); and the Employers' Liability (Compulsory Insurance) Act 1969 (which restricts the defences open to an insurer under compulsory employers' liability insurance policies). The only form of insurance contract which is subject to substantial legislative control is compulsory motor insurance: the Road Traffic Act 1988, which implements various EC Directives on motor insurance, in effect

---

1. See the discussion in chapter 1.

rewrites the policy by allowing third parties to claim under it and deprives the insurer of the right to depend upon policy conditions and other defences in most situations.[2]

The position, therefore, is that, subject to the limited exceptions noted earlier, the legal principles applicable to insurance contracts, are those of the common law. The underlying principles were developed in the days of Lord Mansfield's stewardship of the Court of King's Bench in the second half of the eighteenth century, at a time when the most important forms of insurance were marine and, to a lesser extent, life and fire, and when the policies were almost exclusively commercial in nature. Moreover, insurance activity itself was at a relatively early stage in its development and insurers were perceived to be in need of protection against fraud and sharp practice. It is hardly surprising to find, therefore, that the early common law rules embodied a strict *laissez faire* approach, a process which was developed by nineteenth century judges in accordance with prevailing political philosophy that the existence of competition between enterprises was of itself enough to prevent abuses by any one of them. Consequently, by the time of the evolution of 'consumer' participation in the insurance market in the twentieth century, principles of insurance law had more or less been determined. Although there have been a number of what might be termed 'sympathetic' judicial rulings in favour of consumers in recent years, the general approach of the judiciary has remained one of even-handedness in the application of rules concerning, for example, pre-contract disclosure by the assured and the construction of policy wordings. The perception has been one of unfairness in the law, and it is indeed the case that in many jurisdictions – including some in Continental Europe – legislation has intervened to lay down strict controls over which terms may and may not be included in insurance policies.

## Some features of English insurance law

### Utmost good faith

Any contract which is induced by a false statement is voidable at the instance of the innocent party. This rule applies equally to insurance contracts. However, in insurance law the assured faces the additional obligation to disclose to the insurer all facts material

---

2. See the discussion of motor vehicle insurance in chapter 3.

to the risk prior to the making of the contract. The twin principles of non-disclosure and misrepresentation – collectively referred to as utmost good faith or *uberrima fides* – if broken render the policy voidable and entitle the insurer to avoid the policy *ab initio*, subject to a return of the assured's premium other than in cases of fraud or where the policy entitles the insurer to retain the premium following avoidance. The rules as to utmost good faith are set out in ss 18 to 20 of the Marine Insurance Act 1906, which apply equally outside the marine context.

The insurer has the right to avoid the policy for non-disclosure or misrepresentation of a fact where two requirements, one objective and one subjective, are met. First, looked at in purely objective terms, the fact must be material in that it 'would influence the judgment of a prudent insurer'[3] in accepting the risk or in fixing the premium: whether or not this is the case is to be determined by market evidence. In the leading authority, *Pan Atlantic Insurance Co Ltd v Pine Top Insurance Co Ltd*,[4] the House of Lords, by a 3:2 majority, ruled that the quoted phrase referred not to the final decision which might be reached by a prudent insurer, but rather to a prudent insurer's thought processes, so that the fact need not have a decisive influence on the decision of a prudent insurer. It was subsequently confirmed by the Court of Appeal in *St Paul Fire and Marine Insurance Co (UK) Ltd v McConnell Dowell Constructors Ltd*[5] that a fact is material if a prudent insurer would have wanted to know about it, even though the insurer might have reached the same decision as to accepting the risk and as to premium had it been aware of it. The second, subjective, requirement – recognised by a unanimous House of Lords in *Pan Atlantic* – is that the insurer itself must have been induced to enter into the contract by reason of the assured's breach of duty.

In *Pan Atlantic* there was some disagreement as to whether proof of materiality led to a presumption of inducement in favour of the insurer: Lord Mustill was in favour of such a presumption, whereas Lord Lloyd was against it. The issue was resolved in favour of a presumption of inducement by the Court of Appeal in *St Paul Fire*, where an insurer unable to give evidence as to the

---

3. Marine Insurance Act 1906, ss 18(2) (non-disclosure) and 20(2) (misrepresentation).
4. [1994] 3 All ER 581.
5. [1995] 2 Lloyd's Rep 116.

circumstances in which cover had been granted was able to take advantage of the presumption of inducement. The presumption is not, however, available where the insurer is able to give evidence as to what passed between the parties when the risk was written but has refused to do so, or where it is shown that the insurer was, when the risk was presented to it, not acting in a prudent fashion so that the burden of proving that its judgment was influenced by the presentation of the risk passes to that insurer.[6]

The duty of utmost good faith as applied by the English courts has been heavily criticised by practitioners, academics and judges for its apparent unfairness. The most important objections are the following.

(a) Where the duty is broken, there is an all or nothing remedy, in that the insurer can avoid the entire policy even though the fact misstated or withheld might have had at most a marginal effect on the premium. Other jurisdictions, particularly in Europe, recognise the concept of proportional recovery.

(b) The definition of materiality, by focusing on the insurer rather than the assured, means that the assured has to try to guess exactly what facts a prudent insurer would regard as material. Where the fact relates directly to the risk – the 'physical hazard' – e.g., in the case of life assurance, to the assured's health, occupation or pastimes, no great difficulty arises. However, the law also recognises a second form of material fact, the 'moral hazard', which requires disclosure of rather less obvious matters, such as criminal convictions and past insurance history, including previous refusals to insure and previous claims.

(c) The insurer is entitled to avoid liability despite the fact that the facts misstated or withheld are totally unconnected to the circumstances of the loss.

(d) There is no effective equivalent duty on the insurer to disclose material facts concerning the nature of the cover and the meaning of the policy.[7]

---

6. *Marc Rich & Co AG v Portman* [1996] 1 Lloyd's Rep 630, where it was emphasised that previous imprudence on the part of the insurer is immaterial to this question: the assured must prove imprudence in relation to the risk under consideration.

7. The duty of utmost good faith is bilateral, but as was demonstrated by the complex facts in *La Banque Financière de la Cité SA v Westgate Insurance Co Ltd* [1990] 2 All ER 947, the assured cannot claim damages against the insurer if he finds himself without cover which he expected to exist: the only remedy is recovery of premium, which is likely to be little consolation where the assured has suffered a major, uninsured, loss.

It is only right to point out that in recent years the burdens imposed by the duty of utmost good faith have to some extent been mitigated by the courts. The decision in *Pan Atlantic* itself, by superimposing the requirement that the actual insurer has been induced by the assured's pre-contractual breach of duty, is likely to have some remedial effect, although it may be that the recognition of the presumption of inducement in *St Paul Fire* will largely negative the effects of the need for inducement. Moreover, the courts have in recent years been prepared to expand the notion of waiver of disclosure, by ruling that if an insurer fails to ask obvious questions it thereby waives disclosure of the information which those questions would have elicited.[8] Finally, a series of Court of Appeal decisions has determined that the assured cannot disclose information which is not in the assured's possession, and that information known to the assured's agent is not to be imputed to the assured.[9] Nevertheless, the basic rules remain in force and are capable of producing injustice.

### Warranties

English law has long recognised the concept of the insurance 'promissory warranty', which is an unconditional promise given by the assured at the time the contract is made that facts stated by the assured are true at that time. In some cases, the assured may promise that the facts will remain true for the duration of the contract, in which case the warranty is generally referred to as a 'future warranty'. If the fact is not as stated, or if in the case of a future warranty circumstances change, the assured is in breach of warranty and the insurer is automatically off risk as from the date of the assured's breach.[10] One particularly unfortunate consequence of the automatic termination rule is that if the assured has been in breach of warranty even for a short period, the assured cannot, by repairing the breach, reinstate the risk in the absence of waiver by the insurer.[11] The key feature of the warranty is that the

---

8. As in *GMA v Storebrand* [1995] LRLR 333.
9. The most recent of these cases is *PCW Syndicates v PCW Reinsurers* [1996] 1 Lloyd's Rep 241.
10. These principles are set out in the Marine Insurance Act 1906, ss 33–34, as construed by the House of Lords in *Bank of Nova Scotia v Hellenic Mutual War Risks Association, The Good Luck* [1991] 3 All ER 1. The decision is concerned with marine insurance, but probably applies to all classes of insurance.
11. The only exception is the development by the courts of the concept of the

insurer's rights operate whether or not the fact in question was material to the risk and whether or not the breach of warranty contributed to the loss, and there are numerous English cases in which irrelevant and minor false statements by the assured have precluded recovery by the assured.[12] One long-favoured method of creating warranties has been by means of the 'basis' clause in proposal forms, whereby the assured declares all of the answers to be the basis of the contract: the basis clause converts all proposal form statements, material and immaterial, into warranties.[13] These principles have attracted a good deal of criticism, including from the courts at the highest level,[14] but the common law has survived largely unscathed.

## Meaning of policy wordings

In line with the *laissez faire* attitude which underlies English contract law, the terms of insurance policies are to be given their obvious meaning, however one-sided such meaning might appear to be. As a matter of law a proposer has no right to view the terms of the policy which that proposer is about to enter, and is deemed to have applied for insurance on the insurer's standard terms.[15] It is also the practice of insurers to render the assured's obligations under the policy conditions precedent to the right to recover so that if, for example, the assured fails to comply with a claims obligation which requires notice of loss to be given either immediately or within a fixed period, the insurer is entitled to refuse a late claim even though the delay is short, excusable and has not caused any prejudice to the insurer.[16]

11. *(continued)* suspensory provision', whereby a term is construed not as a warranty but merely as a statement of the circumstances in which the insurer is liable, so that if there is a temporary failure to comply the policy is suspended for that period, but the risk reattaches thereafter: see, e.g., *Provincial Insurance Co Ltd v Morgan* [1933] AC 240.

12. See *Allen v Universal Automobile Insurance* (1933) 45 Ll LR 55: minor discrepancy between the stated and actual price paid by the assured for a car.

13. *Yorkshire Insurance v Campbell* [1917] AC 218 – immaterial misstatement as to the pedigree of a horse: *Dawsons Ltd v Bonnin* [1922] 2 AC 413 – immaterial misstatement as to place in which a lorry was located.

14. See Lord Griffiths in *Forsikringsaktieselskapet Vesta v Butcher* [1989] 1 All ER 402, where the absence of causal connection between breach of warranty and the loss was criticised.

15. *General Accident Insurance Corporation v Cronk* (1901) 17 TLR 333.

16. See, e.g., *Cassel v Lancashire and Yorkshire Accident Insurance Co* (1885) 1 TLR 495; *Pioneer Concrete (UK) Ltd v National Employers Mutual General Insurance Association Ltd* [1985] 2 All ER 395.

## Reform

In the last two decades a number of separate initiatives, two of which have been EC-inspired, have transformed English insurance law as it applies to consumer transactions, particularly as regards the features identified above. The EC initiatives will be considered later in this chapter, and it is first necessary to set out the domestic context in which they have arisen. The key point which emerges from the following account is that EC proposals have been the catalyst for domestic reforms.

### The Statements of Insurance Practice

The first development was the passing of the Unfair Contract Terms Act 1977, an Act which, *inter alia*, requires exclusion clauses contained in consumer contracts and in contracts made in the supplier's standard form to be reasonable.[17] However, insurance contracts were excluded from the Act, in the light of the point made by the insurance industry that requiring the courts to assess the reasonableness of exclusions from coverage would amount to judicial reassessment of the premium: if, for example, a court took the view that it was unreasonable to exclude riot damage from household insurance, the court would in effect be saying that the premium paid by the assured ought to buy more cover than had in fact been granted. The force of this point was accepted and the exemption was conferred.

The insurance industry nevertheless had to pay a price for this concession, that price being an understanding that some degree of self-regulation would be introduced to mitigate the more extreme effects of the common law. Accordingly, in 1977 the Association of British Insurers (ABI) adopted two Statements of Insurance Practice, one for long-term (life) policies and one for general (non-life) insurance. The Statements were revised in 1986. The Statements apply to policyholders resident in the UK and insured in their private capacity only, and have the following effects.

(a) When completing the proposal form, the assured should be required to answer questions only to the best of their knowledge and belief: an insurer should not, for example, be entitled to rely upon a statement that the assured is in good

---

17. Unfair Contract Terms Act 1977, ss 3 and 11.

health when in fact the assured had an undiscoverable illness. Questions are, as far as possible, not to extend to matters beyond the assured's knowledge or experience. The assured is to be advised to retain a copy of all documentation containing information given to the insurer, and the insurer is to retain a copy of the proposal form for the assured's inspection on request. The defence of misrepresentation is in general not to be pleaded unless the assured has acted fraudulently or negligently.

(b) As regards disclosure of material facts, the insurer should ask express questions wherever possible, and should include a clear warning on the proposal form that the assured is under a duty to disclose all other material facts. An insurer is not to reject a claim based on non-disclosure where the assured could not reasonably have been expected to have disclosed the fact in issue.

(c) Answers on proposal forms should not be converted into warranties by the use of 'basis of the contract' clauses. Warranties are to be created individually and expressly. Where the assured is in breach of warranty, the insurer is to deny liability only where there is a causal connection between the breach of warranty and the circumstances of the loss.

(d) Policy terms should be readily available to a potential assured, thereby mitigating the common law principle that a proposer for insurance is deemed to be applying for the insurer's standard terms whether or not the assured has seen them. Insurers are also encouraged to use clearer and more explicit documentation.

(e) A claims notification clause is to give the assured a reasonable time in which to report and make a claim. The Statements thus prohibit the use of fixed-term notification clauses or 'immediate' notification clauses, both of which have in many reported cases deprived the assured of what was otherwise a perfectly good claim. Claims are to be paid without delay.

(f) On renewal (which, in non-life cases, creates a fresh contract) the assured is to be warned that the duty of utmost good faith reattaches for the purposes of the renewal.

### The Insurance Ombudsman Bureau

The Statements of Insurance Practice are not legally binding, and received early criticism on the basis that there was no method of ensuring that their terms were adhered to by insurers. This deficiency was remedied in 1981 by the establishment of the Insurance Ombudsman Bureau (IOB), by a small group of insurers operating on a voluntary basis. Part of the impetus for the setting up of the IOB was a Law Commission proposal for the modification of the law of disclosure and warranties, which had itself been prompted by EC moves – subsequently abandoned – towards insurance contract law harmonisation. Over the succeeding years, virtually all major insurers, including Lloyd's, have joined the IOB scheme, although in 1994, on the formation of the Personal Investment Authority (PIA) as the regulatory body for life offices under the Financial Services Act 1986, the IOB's life jurisdiction has been transferred to the PIA Ombudsman, who operates on a similar basis.

The IOB's jurisdiction extends only to consumer assureds. On receiving a complaint by an assured, and being satisfied that the matter has been considered at the highest levels by the insurer, the IOB may become involved, initially as a conciliator and ultimately as an adjudicator with the jurisdiction to make an award binding on the insurer[18] of up to £100,000. In 1995, the IOB received some 50,000 written and telephone inquiries, and handled some 8,000 cases resulting from inquiries. The IOB is charged with the duty of ensuring that insurers adhere to 'good insurance practice', and to this extent is free to depart from strict rules of law where these operate unfairly. The IOB has developed a substantial jurisprudence on matters which have yet to come before the courts,[19] and in at least one situation – that of the meaning of 'reasonable care' obligations imposed on the assured – has influenced subsequent judicial developments.[20] While the IOB does not operate on the basis of precedent, its decisions are made by lawyers and its publication of annual reports, quarterly case reports and a bound digest of decisions points towards the development of formal principles.

18. But not on the assured, who has the right to reject the adjudication and go to court.
19. For example the development of rules for determining the measure of indemnity where one piece of a matching set is damaged: the assured will normally be awarded one-half of the value of the entire set.
20. In *Sofi v Prudential Assurance* [1993] 2 Lloyd's Rep 559 the Court of Appeal, quoting the IOB's annual reports, confirmed that a reasonable care clause merely requires the assured to avoid recklessness in their conduct.

# The Commission's draft harmonisation directives

## The proposals

At an early stage in the process of harmonising the regulation of insurers, facilitating the free movement of insurance services across national boundaries,[21] the Commission came to the view that it was necessary also to harmonise various aspects of substantive insurance law, for two reasons. First, the laying down of a common set of rules would mean that a potential assured, in choosing between insurance policies offered by insurers from different EC jurisdictions, would not be influenced by the fact that alien principles of law would be applicable to the policy in the event that the assured opted for an insurer located outside the place of the assured's own domicile. Secondly, it was thought necessary on pure consumer protection grounds to provide certain minimum safeguards for assureds, particularly as the harmonisation of regulation was inevitably going to lead to the abolition of the right of a member state – then a common feature of Continental but not UK regulation – to impose 'material' control over the policy terms and premium levels offered by insurers.

The first proposal for a Council Directive on the co-ordination of laws, regulations and administrative provisions relating to insurance contracts was published in July 1979,[22] and was subsequently revised by a second version published in December 1980.[23] Agreement on the Directives could not, however, be reached at Council of Ministers' level, and the proposal was shelved until its formal abandonment in 1994. In its place, the Second Generation of Insurance Directives adopted the concept of laying down choice of law rules for risks located within the EC, the basic principle being that the assured is entitled to the benefit of their domestic law (unless that law permits contracting out) irrespective of the nationality of the insurer. The content of the proposals is nevertheless of interest, and, as will be seen below, has had some impact on the development of English law. In the following paragraphs, references to the draft Directive are to the 1980 revised version unless otherwise stated.

21. This process is traced in chapter 1.
22. 10 July 1979.
23. 30 December 1980.

## Scope

Article 1 of the draft Directive excluded life insurance, and while the proposal was not specifically limited to private or consumer assureds, many forms of commercial risk – including transport and credit policies – were excluded from it.

### Disclosure of information to the assured

Article 2 was concerned with ensuring that the assured received adequate information as to the content of the policy after the making of the contract. The assured was to receive, without delay after the making of the contract or of an agreement for temporary cover, a document containing the name and address of the insurer, the nature of the cover provided, the sum insured and excluded risks, details as to the amount and payment of the premium, and the duration of the contract. Revisions in any of these matters were to be notified to the assured. The relevant information was to be provided to the assured in the language of the place of the assured's habitual residence. There are no rules of this type operative in English law, and indeed, marine insurance aside, there is no obligation on the insurer to provide a policy to the assured at all.

### Pre-contract disclosure

Perhaps the most wide-ranging changes, at least as far as the UK was concerned, appeared in article 3 of the draft Directive. To some extent, the proposals reflected English law. The assured was under a duty to disclose material facts to the insurer, the test being whether the assured was reasonably aware of the fact (a matter not set out in the Marine Insurance Act 1906 but nevertheless implicit in English law) and whether a prudent insurer would have been influenced by it (consistently with English law).

The differences arise as regards remedies. Under the original draft of the Directive, if the assured failed to disclose material facts, either because the assured was not aware of them or did not believe them to be material, the insurer was not entitled to terminate the contract but rather had the right, on becoming aware of the facts, to propose an amendment to the policy which the assured could accept or reject: only on rejection of the amendment did the insurer have the right to terminate the policy.

However, if the assured's breach of duty had been the result of 'improper conduct' on their part (presumably, either fraud or gross negligence), the insurer was given the right either to terminate the policy or to propose an amendment to it, which could be either accepted or rejected by the assured. In either case, prior to the termination of the policy the insurer was liable for accrued claims in the proportion that the premium paid bore to the premium that would have been paid with full disclosure. The effect of the 1979 draft was, therefore, to remove the insurer's right to avoid *ab initio* where the assured had not been guilty of fraud or the equivalent, and to replace that right with a lesser right to propose changes to cover or to premium.

All of this was watered down in the 1980 draft, and distinctions were drawn between innocent, negligent and fraudulent failures to make full disclosure. Following an innocent failure to disclose by the assured, the insurer was given a period of two months from discovering the fact either to propose an amendment to the policy or to give notice of termination. In the case of a proposed amendment, the assured was given one month to consider the amendment, and if it was rejected or not responded to the insurer had the right to terminate the contract by notice within a further period of eight days. In the case of notice of termination being given, termination was to take effect one month in consumer cases (fifteen days in other cases) after notice had been given. Any claim arising during these consideration periods had to be met in full, and in the absence of a claim the assured was entitled to a return of the premium representing the unexpired part of the policy. By contrast, if the assured had acted negligently, the same principles applied, with two differences: the insurer's notice of termination could take effect after fifteen days in all cases, and if a loss occurred prior to termination the insurer was liable only for that proportion of the loss which the premium actually paid bore to the premium which would have been paid on full disclosure. Proof by the insurer that the risk was uninsurable discharged it from all liability for losses in this period. Different principles applied where the assured had failed to make full disclosure with an intent to deceive (fraud). Here, the insurer was given two months to terminate the contract: it could not face liability for losses occurring prior to termination, and the premiums were to be forfeited by the assured.

Article 3 equally permitted the assured to terminate or to

propose an amendment to the policy where facts not known by the assured subsequently became apparent.

## Increase of risk

In English law, where circumstances change and the risk increases after the making of the policy, the assured is under no obligation to inform the insurer of the changes and the insurer equally has no right to charge a higher premium. This is subject to any express agreement to the contrary, and in particular a future warranty may have the effect of determining the risk automatically where the risk has increased. Article 3 of the Directive would have obliged the assured to notify the insurer of an increase in the risk but only where such information had been requested and where the increase would have been permanent, appreciable and would have led to an increase in premium. A non-fraudulent failure to notify conferred upon the insurer the right within two months to propose an amendment to the policy or to terminate it. In the case of a proposed amendment, the assured was given a month to accept or reject, and a rejection or failure to respond permitted the insurer to terminate the policy within a further eight days. In the case of a decision by the insurer to terminate, rather than propose an amendment to, the policy termination was effective after fifteen days from the receipt of the insurer's notice. As was the case under art 3, losses prior to termination were to be paid on a proportionate basis. A fraudulent failure to notify conferred upon the insurer the right to terminate, to retain the assured's premiums and to escape liability for any loss occurring after the risk had increased. It will readily be appreciated that these provisions would have required significant changes to the English law of warranties, in particular by preventing the insurer from coming off risk automatically for any alteration of risk even if immaterial to the policy.

## Reduction of risk

Article 5 would have conferred upon the assured a right not recognised by English law. Under this provision, where the risk had diminished, the assured had the right to ask for a reduction in the premium, and if the insurer refused the assured could give notice of termination and recover the unexpired portion of the premium. The English position is that once the risk has commenced, any reduction in it, and indeed the elimination of it, does not entitle the assured to any return of premium, on the basis that there can be restitution only for a total failure of consideration, i.e., where the risk has never been run at all.[24]

### Payment of the premium

Article 6 conferred another right not recognised by English law, namely, the right of an assured who has not paid a renewal premium when it was due to escape the consequences of non-payment (normally forfeiture) until the assured has received a notice giving fifteen days during which to make payment. The common law does not protect the assured against forfeiture for late payment.

### Mitigation of loss

It is almost universal practice in marine insurance for the policy to contain a 'suing and labouring' clause, whereby the assured falls under a duty to take reasonable steps to prevent or mitigate loss, and the insurer is under a corresponding duty to indemnify the assured for the reasonable costs incurred in doing so in addition to any sums due under the policy itself. Various aspects of the duty await judicial determination, and in particular it is not clear whether the assured loses the entire indemnity on failing to sue and labour, or merely that part of it caused by the assured's inaction.[25] It is also uncertain how the duty to sue and labour relates to the principle that mere negligence on the assured's part does not deprive the assured of a right to indemnification.[26] It has not been the practice in England for suing and labouring provisions to be used in non-marine insurance, and there is no real authority on the extent to which the common law requires an assured to take steps to avoid or mitigate the loss.[27]

24. *Tyrie v Fletcher* (1774) 2 Cowp 666, codified in the Marine Insurance Act 1906, s 84.
25. *Noble Resources Ltd and Unirise Development Ltd v George Albert Greenwood, The Vasso* [1993] 2 Lloyd's Rep 309 (partial recovery); *National Oilwell UK Ltd v Davy Offshore Ltd* [1993] 2 Lloyd's Rep 582 (no recovery – loss caused by assured).
26. Various unconvincing explanations have been put forward. See in particular *The Gold Sky* [1972] 2 QB 611.
27. The corresponding question – whether, in the absence of a suing and labouring clause or equivalent provision, an insurer is required to indemnify an assured for the cost of steps taken to avoid a loss – has been answered in the negative by the Court of Appeal in *Yorkshire Water v Sun Alliance* 1996, unreported.

Article 7 of the draft Directive would have introduced a modified form of suing and labouring into the general law. The assured had to take reasonable steps to avoid or reduce the consequences of a loss (wording which made it clear that the assured's negligence leading up to the loss could not prejudice the claim). The costs of mitigation were to be borne by the insurer in addition to sums due under the policy. Failure to mitigate, unless fraudulent, was not to prejudice the claim, but was to render the assured liable in damages to the insurer for the loss caused to it: this is in line with the more liberal view of suing and labouring referred to earlier.

### Notice of loss and other co-operation

By virtue of art 8, the assured was to be under an obligation to notify losses to the insurer, and to provide such proofs as the insurer might require, but the policy could not require more than notice or action within a reasonable time. This provision reflected the ABI's Statements of Insurance Practice. Article 8 went on to provide that failure to notify in time would not have discharged the insurer, but would have rendered the assured liable to the insurer for loss suffered by it, although in the case of fraud by the assured the insurer was to be regarded as discharged from all liability.

### Termination and duration

Under art 10, policies were to specify the circumstances in which they could come to an end. Article 10 further set out the circumstances in which the insurer could terminate the policy prior to its natural lapse. The insurer was entitled to terminate early and without notice only in the case of fraud, and in other cases termination could be effected by the insurer only on fifteen days' notice. The common law was silent on these issues.

## The UK's response

As has been demonstrated, the draft Directive would have conferred upon assureds far greater rights than those recognised by the common law. In May 1978 the Lord Chancellor, anticipating from early private drafts the adoption of a Directive along the lines set out above, asked the Law Commission to produce a report on the areas covered by the proposals, including utmost good faith, warranties and change of risk. The Law Commission responded with a Working Paper published in February 1979[28] which contained bold proposals for modification of English law. In outline:

(a) As regards utmost good faith:
  (i) the duty of disclosure was to continue but in modified form;
  (ii) where the assured had completed a proposal form, there was no obligation to disclose any information other than that specifically requested on the form, thereby in effect abolishing the duty in the absence of express questions – the only exception arose where the assured deliberately withheld material facts;
  (iii) information sought by express questions would be presumed, but not conclusively so, to be material, so that misstatement would *prima facie* give the insurer the right to avoid the policy; even where express questions were asked, the assured was to be obliged to answer questions only to the best of their knowledge and belief;
  (iv) where the assured had not completed a proposal form, they would have to disclose facts which a prudent *assured* as well as a prudent insurer would regard as material, so that the duty remained but with a test of materiality more favourable to the assured.

(b) As regards warranties:
  (i) warranties should be permitted to continue to exist, but in modified form;
  (ii) a term could operate as a warranty only if it was material to the risk, the burden of proving materiality resting on the insurer;
  (iii) the insurer would be entitled to plead breach of warranty as a defence only if the breach had some causal connection with the loss.

These proposals were put out to consultation, and were given a frosty reception, particularly by the insurance industry, for overreacting to what were admittedly injustices in the pre-existing

---

28. Law Commission Working Paper No 73: *Insurance Law: Non-Disclosure and Breach of Warranty.*

law. Accordingly, when the Law Commission produced its final report in October 1980,[29] shortly before the publication by the European Commission of its weaker revised second draft, the Law Commission's proposals and the appended draft Bill had been modified considerably. Turning first to utmost good faith, the Law Commission took the view that there should be a duty of disclosure whether or not the assured had completed a proposal form, but that the test of materiality should be modified to provide that a fact would have to be disclosed if it was regarded as material both by a prudent assured and a prudent insurer. The proposals in the original draft Directive requiring proportional payment by the insurer other than in cases of fraud were rejected, and it will have been noted above that proportionality was subsequently all but abandoned by the European Commission in the final draft of its Directive published some two months later.

Turning to warranties, the Law Commission reaffirmed the views which it had expressed in the Working Paper, and proposed that a term should be capable of constituting a warranty only where it was material to the risk and that a breach of warranty should entitle an insurer to reject a claim only where the breach was causative of the loss. The Law Commission did not, however, condemn the use of 'basis of the contract' clauses in proposal forms as a means of creating warranties.

### Subsequent developments

The shelving and subsequent abandonment by the European Commission of its draft Directive meant that English amending legislation was not required as a matter of EC law. Nevertheless, the UK government prepared a Bill implementing with modifications the Law Commission's final proposals, but this was never formally published. Instead, the insurance industry agreed to increased self-regulation, and this led to the establishment of the Insurance Ombudsman Bureau in 1981 and the adoption of revised Statements of Insurance Practice in 1986. Consequently, while the EC's brief flirtation with substantive harmonisation did not have any direct impact on the law, it had a major impact on consumer protection through self-regulation.

---

29. Law Commission Report No 104: *Insurance Law: Non-Disclosure and Breach of Warranty.*

# Control of unfair terms in consumer contracts

## The Unfair Contract Terms Directive 1993

In 1993 the Council of Ministers adopted Directive 93/13 on unfair terms in consumer contracts. The Directive had two objectives: to secure the single market by providing that consumers had the same minimum level of protection against unfair terms in sale of goods and supply of services contracts wherever in the EC the contract was made; and to provide, in accordance with the principles contained in the Maastricht Treaty's amendments to the Treaty of Rome, a high level of consumer protection on general policy grounds. The Directive is similar in its impact to the UK's pre-existing Unfair Contract Terms Act 1977, but there are a number of important differences between the two. Perhaps the most important for present purposes is that the Directive, unlike the 1977 Act, does not exclude insurance contracts from its scope.

The Directive was implemented in the UK by the Unfair Terms in Consumer Contracts Regulations 1994,[30] with effect from 1 July 1995.[31] Despite the substantial overlaps between the 1977 Act and the Directive, the government chose not to repeal the 1977 Act and to produce a single piece of legislation which implemented the Directive and retained the additional features of the 1977 Act. Instead, the 1977 Act was left intact and the Directive was implemented, more or less verbatim, by a separate set of Regulations. The result is that, as regards most consumer contracts, two pieces of legislation govern the same matter, whereas commercial contracts are governed exclusively by the 1977 Act. However, in the light of the exclusion of insurance from the 1977 Act, as far as insurance is concerned, only the 1994 Regulations are relevant. In the following discussion of the Regulations, their insurance application only is considered.

## The 1994 Regulations and insurance

### General scope

The 1994 Regulations apply to the terms of a contract of sale or supply made between a seller or supplier acting for purposes relating to their business, and a consumer who is a natural person

30. SI 1994 No 3159.  31. This was six months late.

45

(i.e., not a company or a partnership) acting for purposes outside their business.[32] It will be appreciated that all consumer insurances are within the Regulations. The effect of the Regulations is to render void as against the consumer any severable term which is unfair:[33] if the term is not severable from the rest of the contract, the entire contract is apparently negatived. In addition, the Director General of Fair Trading is empowered by the Regulations to prevent the use of specific unfair terms by groups of suppliers, if necessary by seeking an injunction against such use.[34]

Contracting out of the Regulations is prohibited.[35]

### The criteria of unfairness

A term is potentially unfair if it satisfies each of three criteria. First, the term must be one which has not been *individually negotiated*,[36] i.e., where the term 'has been drafted in advance and the consumer has not been able to influence the substance of the term'.[37] Mere tinkering with the wording following discussion with the assured will not suffice to take the term outside the Regulations, as it is the 'substance' of the term rather than its actual phraseology which is referred to by the Regulations, and in any event the burden of proving individual negotiation is borne by the insurer.[38] Where, therefore, a consumer is presented with a standard form insurance wording and does not have the opportunity to negotiate its terms, this criterion will have been met for the entire contract. If a term is individually negotiated, the Regulations continue to apply to the remainder of the contract.[39]

Secondly, the insurer's reliance on the term must be *contrary to the requirement of good faith*.[40] The concept of dealing in good faith is a feature of Continental contract law, but does not form any part of general English contract law. This concept is, therefore, carefully defined by the Regulations. In determining whether the insurer's reliance on a term would be contrary to good faith, the court must take into account four factors, although other factors may also be considered and the weight to be given to them is a matter for the court. The factors are:[41]

---

32. Reg 2.  33. Reg 5.  34. Reg 8.  35. Reg 7.  36. Reg 3(1).
37. Reg 3(2).  38. Reg 3(5).  39. Reg 3(4).  40. Reg 4(1).
41. Sched 2, which is more than reminiscent of the criteria of fairness applicable under Sched 2 to the Unfair Contract Terms Act 1977.

(a)  the relative strength of the parties' bargaining positions;
(b)  whether the assured was offered any inducement to agree to the term under dispute;
(c)  whether the policy was supplied to the special order of the assured;
(d)  whether and the extent to which the insurer has dealt fairly and equitably with the assured.

Thirdly, the term must result in a *'significant imbalance in the parties' rights and obligations under the contract to the detriment of the consumer'*.[42]

### Assessment of unfairness

Where the criteria of unfairness have been found to exist, it remains necessary for the court to determine whether or not the term is actually unfair in the circumstances. The Regulations provide that this exercise is to be conducted by the court 'taking into account the nature of the goods or services for which the contract was concluded and referring, as at the time of the conclusion of the contract, to all circumstances attending the conclusion of the contract and to all other terms of the contract'.[43] This test, which is similar to the general test for reasonableness laid down by the Unfair Contract Terms Act 1977, requires the court to look at the situation when the contract was made and not at how the contract operated subsequently.

### The 'core' provision

It was stated earlier that the insurance industry secured its exemption from the Unfair Contracts Terms Act 1977 on the basis that allowing a court to assess the fairness of exclusion clauses would be tantamount to asking it to perform an underwriting role and to assess what would be a fair premium for the risks actually covered by the policy. This objection may or may not be valid,[44]

---

42. Reg 4(1).    43. Reg 4(2).
44. It might be argued against this that every exclusion clause in every class of contract has an impact upon the price paid by the consumer, as the exclusion determines the degree of risk which the seller or supplier is prepared to bear for its own account: the point just happens to be rather more obvious in the insurance context.

but was accepted by the Directive and has found its way into what has become known as the 'core provision' of the Regulations.[45] Under this provision, a court is not permitted to assess the fairness of any term which either (a) defines the subject matter of the contract or (b) concerns the adequacy of the price or remuneration, as against the goods or services sold or supplied. As far as insurance is concerned, therefore, the insuring clause and the exceptions clause are probably sacrosanct, and the Regulations are concerned only with ancillary terms, e.g., notice of loss and co-operation provisions, obligations imposed on the assured during the currency of the policy, and restrictions on bringing judicial proceedings. The core provision is nevertheless restricted in one important aspect, in that it provides relief only where the clause in question is expressed in 'plain, intelligible language'. An insurer who uses obscure phraseology to delimit the scope of cover may find that the term is subject to the full force of the Regulations, and that an attempt to exclude a particular form of liability may be negatived on the ground that the entire clause is to be regarded as void. It might be added that any ambiguity in the insuring clause itself is within the Regulations, as these go on to provide that any term in a consumer contract which has not been individually negotiated and is not in plain, intelligible language is to be given 'the interpretation most favourable to the consumer'.[46] Ambiguous coverage may, therefore, be wider than was intended by the insurer.

One final point may be made here. Uncertainty as to the meaning of insuring clauses and exceptions can arise in one of two ways. First, the language may be confused and ambiguous: it is clear that this is the prime target of the Regulations. Secondly, the language may be plain, but may be subject to unexpected interpretation. For example, ordinary English words such as 'theft', 'riot', 'fire' and 'explosion' have all acquired technical meanings when used in insurance policies. A side-effect of the Regulations may, therefore, be to prevent insurers from relying upon narrow technical meanings of ordinary English words: this

---

45. Reg 3(3).
46. Reg 6. This is *prima facie* a codification of the old common law *contra proferentem* rule of construction, but goes somewhat further in the insurance context as there is some authority for the proposition that *contra proferentem* will not apply in an insurance case to wording which was proposed originally by a broker, although *quaere* whether such a term is to be regarded as 'individually negotiated'.

will depend upon whether the courts will regard ordinary words as not being plain and intelligible.

### When are insurance terms likely to be unfair?

The Directive contains a helpful illustrative list of terms which might be expected to fall foul of the fairness requirement. This list, which is neither exhaustive nor conclusive, and for these reasons has rather unfairly been dubbed the 'Grey List', is reproduced in the Regulations.[47] No less than sixteen different terms are identified, and those likely to be relevant to insurance are set out below. A term is at risk if it has the object or effect of:

(1) making performance of the contract subject to a condition under the insurer's exclusive control;

(2) permitting the insurer to retain the premium if the assured fails to proceed – by analogy, a clause which permits retention of the premium where the policy is avoided for the assured's breach of duty may, assuming that the assured has been honest, be open to challenge;

(3) authorising the insurer in its discretion to cancel the contract while not conferring an equivalent right on the assured – it might be possible to argue that even a bilateral right to terminate is unfair, if the insurer is free to exercise that right when a loss appears to be in the offing;

(4) automatically extending the policy unless the assured has reasonable opportunity to determine the policy;

(5) binding the assured to terms which the assured had no reasonable opportunity to see prior to the making of the contract – it might be thought that insurance contracts are particularly vulnerable here;

(6) enabling the insurer unilaterally to alter the terms of the policy;

(7) limiting the insurer's obligation to be bound by the acts of its authorised agents. A clause which deems the insurer's agent to be that of the assured if the agent completes the proposal form would seem to fall into this category:

(8) obliging the assured to perform despite the insurer's breach;

(9) excluding or hindering the consumer's access to legal redress –

47. Sched 2.

an arbitration clause would in principle be caught by this provision.[48]

## Assessment

It is unlikely that the Unfair Contracts Terms Directive and the implementing UK Regulations will have any significant effect upon the insurance industry. As the controls apply only to consumer contracts, they merely replicate one element of the self-regulatory principles established in the Statements of Insurance Practice and in the jurisprudence of the Insurance Ombudsman Bureau. It is nevertheless satisfying to have the force of law, and possible administrative assistance, available to consumers.

---

48. Arbitration clauses are at the time of writing prohibited in consumer contracts by the Consumer Arbitration Agreements Act 1988. That Act is repealed, from a date to be appointed, by the Arbitration Act 1996. Ss 89 to 91 of the 1996 Act merely state that consumer arbitration agreements are governed by the 1994 Regulations, with the modifications that: (a) corporate consumers are protected; and (b) the Secretary of State has the power to confine the Regulations to below certain financial limits, generally expected to be the county court limits.

# CHAPTER THREE

# Motor insurance

## The EC's programme

Motor vehicle insurance has been the subject of a comprehensive harmonisation programme within the European Community. Prior to this programme, member states had individually required road users to carry insurance against liability, although the schemes operated by each of the states were different in terms both of the risks which had to be covered by compulsory insurance and the amount of insurance required. The diversity created obvious obstacles to persons wishing to drive in different member states, thereby hindering both the free movement of commercial vehicles and tourist activities. A related problem was that a person injured in a motor vehicle accident outside their own member state might face immense difficulties in obtaining a judgment backed by insurance in another member state. It was accordingly necessary for the EC to address the possibility of creating a harmonised system of compulsory liability insurance which facilitated free movement and which guaranteed recovery to persons injured abroad.

An additional problem was that, as regards compulsory insurance, some member states imposed additional regulatory obligations upon insurers seeking authorisation to offer such business. The result was that it was not at the outset possible to obtain agreement between member states to include compulsory insurance in the Insurance Directives providing for free movement of services and the right of establishment, as discussed in chapter 1.

It will be seen, therefore, that the EC has been required to adopt a multi-pronged approach to compulsory insurance in general and motor vehicle insurance in particular. The legislation adopted by the EC, which is considered in detail in this chapter, may be summarised as follows.

(1) EC law requires that a person insured in their home state against driving liabilities is insured in all other member states under that domestic policy.
(2) EC law provides that compulsory insurance of motor vehicle liabilities is, subject to minor derogations, the same throughout the EC.
(3) The Single European Licence applicable to insurance companies authorised in their home states extends to motor vehicle insurance.

# Recognition of policies issued in other member states

### The Green Card Scheme

The United Nations has, since 1949[1] operated a 'Green Card' scheme open for adoption by European nations. Under this scheme, a person insured to drive a motor vehicle in their home country and in possession of a Green Card issued by their insurers under the authority of the national association of motor insurers (in the UK, the Motor Insurers Bureau, established in 1946), could use that Green Card to drive a vehicle in any other state with which reciprocal arrangements had been made. The UK acceded to the scheme in 1968, and published implementing Regulations in that year. The present Regulations, replacing earlier versions, are the Motor Vehicles (International Motor Insurance Card) Regulations 1971,[2] which set out the form which a card must take to be valid in the UK and which provide that a Green Card is to have effect as though it were a certificate of insurance issued under the Road Traffic Act 1988. In the event of any accident covered by a compulsory policy, the claim is made against and is satisfied by the UK Motor Insurers Bureau in accordance with the 1988 Act,

---

[1.] By virtue of a recommendation dated 25 January 1949 of the Road Transport Committee of the Inland Transport Committee of the United Nations Economic Commission for Europe.
[2.] SI 1971 No 792.

and the Bureau in turn seeks indemnification from the Motor Insurers Bureau of the driver's home state.

The Green Card Scheme became the starting point for the EC's ultimate objective of freedom of cross-border transfer movement. Council Directive 72/166[3] drew a distinction between vehicles normally based in an EC territory and vehicles normally based outside the EC.[4] In the latter case, the Green Card scheme was to continue in respect of vehicles entering the EC, pending bilateral mutual recognition agreements to the contrary.[5] By contrast, in the case of EC vehicles, the Directive laid down in art 3 an obligation (of, at that stage, undefined scope[6]) on each member state to impose a liability insurance requirement in respect of the use of vehicles both in its own territory and in the territories of all other member states. In the event of an accident in a host territory, the host state's Motor Insurers Bureau was required to obtain details of the insurance vehicle's insurance coverage and to inform the Motor Insurers Bureau of the state in which the vehicle was normally based. A Green Card was still required, but art 2 of the Directive provided that, following an appropriate agreement between the Motor Insurers Bureaux of the member states providing for payment of claims by the Bureau of the state in which the accident occurred, the authorities of the member states would refrain from making systematic checks on EC vehicles entering their territories. Border controls were, on this basis, to be discontinued once an EC-wide system based on the host state indemnifying victims had been agreed. The UK's response was to introduce legislation permitting, in place of a Green Card, an insurance policy issued within the EC and other countries with which reciprocal arrangements existed, to be given as evidence of insurance coverage in the event of an accusation that a vehicle is or has been driven without insurance.[7]

Following Directive 72/166 a series of agreements between

---

3. On the approximation of the laws of the member states relating to insurance against civil liability in respect of the use of motor vehicles, and to the enforcement of the obligation to insure against such liability.

4. The distinction is based on the place of issue of the registration plate: art 1. It was held in Case C-73/92 *Fournier v van Werven*, unreported, that a registration plate must have been lawfully issued for it to qualify under the Directive.

5. Art 7.

6. The scope of compulsory insurance was later to be defined in the Second Motor Insurance Directive, Directive 84/5, and the Third Motor Insurance Directive, Directive 90/232.

7. Motor Vehicles (Third Party Risks) Regulations 1972, SI 1972 No 1217, reg 6.

national Motor Insurers Bureaux of the EC countries and between those Bureaux and those of other European countries was concluded. Under those agreements, and in accordance with the principles of the Green Card scheme, the Bureau of the state in which any accident occurs (the 'handling bureau') becomes responsible for settling the victim's loss, and the handling bureau is then entitled to be indemnified by the Bureau of the place in which the vehicle is normally based (the 'paying bureau'). The various agreements were consolidated into one single agreement, the Multilateral Guarantee Agreement beween National Insurers Bureaux, signed on 15 March 1991, following which the European Commission adopted a consolidated decision[8] dispensing with border and other checks on the insurance position of vehicles normally based in any state which is party to the Agreement. The parties to the Multilateral Guarantee Agreement are the EC member states, Hungary, the Czech Republic, Norway, Slovakia and Iceland.[9] The EC structure has, therefore, removed an important administrative barrier to the free movement of transport across national boundaries.

## The single EC policy

The concept of mutual recognition of insurance obtained elsewhere in the EC has been taken to its inevitable conclusion by the Third Motor Insurance Directive, Directive 90/232.[10] Under art 2 of this Directive, member states were required to take all necessary steps to ensure that all compulsory insurance policies against civil liability arising out of the use of vehicles cover, on the basis of a single premium, the entire territory of the EC. Moreover, the level of cover provided must be that required by the domestic law of the relevant member state or that of the member state in which the vehicle is normally based, whichever is higher. The effect of art 2 is, therefore, to require the insurer to meet the liability of the assured under the law of the place in which the accident occurs, even though the cover required is more extensive than the law of the assured's home state. This article was

---

8. Decision 91/323/EEC.
9. Iceland was added by Decision 93/43/EEC following its accession to the Agreement.
10. Third Council Directive on the approximation of the laws of the member states relating to insurance against civil liability in respect of the use of motor vehicles.

implemented by amendments to the Road Traffic Act 1988. Section 145(3)(aa) of the Act[11] now provides that a compulsory motor policy must, in the case of a vehicle normally based in the territory of another member state, insure the assured against liability as assessed by UK law, and s 145(3)(b) now provides that a compulsory policy in respect of a vehicle normally based in the UK must insure the assured against any liability which may be incurred in the UK or the state in which the accident occurred.

Directive 72/166, art 3(2) further states that in the case of any loss or injury suffered by an EC national during a direct journey between two EC states, in a territory where there is no Motor Insurers Bureau, the loss or injury is to be covered in accordance with the internal laws on compulsory insurance in force in the member state in whose territory the vehicle is normally based. This provision appears not to have been specifically implemented in the UK.

## The scope of compulsory motor insurance

### Risks to be covered

*The Directives*

The first steps towards harmonisation of compulsory motor insurance were taken in Directive 72/166, art 3, which requires all member states to impose compulsory insurance to cover civil liability in respect of the use of vehicles where such use caused 'any loss or injury'. The forms of loss or injury to be covered were at that stage left to member states, and the UK retained, in the Road Traffic Act 1972, the position which had existed since the Road Traffic Act 1930 by confining compulsory cover to death or personal injury, in both cases to an unlimited amount. Article 4 permits member states, in their discretion, to derogate from the general principle of compulsory insurance in cases specified by them, provided that compensation is available to the victims of road users not exempted from the compulsory insurance requirement.

The scope of art 3 was defined by subsequent Directives. Article

---

11. Inserted by the Motor Vehicles (Compulsory Insurance) Regulations 1992, SI 1992 No 3036.

1(1), (2) of Directive 84/5 provides that policies are to cover both death and personal injury for a minimum amount of 350,000 ecu per victim, and property damage for a minimum amount of 100,000 ecu per claim irrespective of the number of victims. In the case of death or personal injury, insurance has to cover passengers other than the driver (Directive 90/232, art 1) and members of the driver's family (Directive 84/5, art 3). UK legislation has, as described below, been amended accordingly.

It is to be emphasised that the Directives are concerned only with third party liability, as opposed to first party loss. It is up to a vehicle owner to decide whether to insure against some or all forms or amounts of damage to the vehicle and indeed to the owner. Where a policy does cover both first and third party losses, it will be seen that the effect of the Directives is to regulate the scope of the policy as regards third party insurance, but to leave entirely to domestic law the scope of first party cover provided by the policy. Accordingly, if in a single accident there are both first and third party losses, the insurer may be required under the Directives to pay the third party claim while having a defence to the first party claim.

### UK reception

The changes required by the Directives were initially introduced in the UK by a statutory instrument amending the Road Traffic Act 1972, but the provisions were later recast and codified in Part VI of the Road Traffic Act 1988, which has itself been amended to take account of subsequent EC developments. The key provision is s 143(1), (2) of the Road Traffic Act 1988, which makes it a criminal offence for a person to 'use' or to 'cause or permit' another person to use, a vehicle on a road where liability insurance meeting the requirements of the Act is not in force. The word 'use' reflects the wording of Directive 72/166, art 3, and has been held by the English courts to refer to control: on this basis, and leaving aside the obvious primary use of a vehicle as driving, a vehicle may be in use by its owner even if it is parked and immobilised[12] and in appropriate circumstances a passenger may be treated as the user if the passenger is participating in driving.[13] The offence is strict,

---

12. Illustrative of the authorities on this point is *Williams v Jones* [1975] RTR 433.
13. This point was at one time relevant for the reason that passengers who were also users were excluded from coverage under the Motor Insurers Bureau

although a person who did not know and had no reason to believe that the vehicle was uninsured has a defence.[14] The offence of causing or permitting uninsured use – which has always been included in the legislation – goes further than EC law requires, and may be committed by a person who allows the use of their vehicle rather than merely facilitating such use, e.g., by selling it to an uninsured person.[15] The offence may apparently be committed even by an owner who is under the mistaken belief that the person whom the owner has authorised to use the vehicle is insured.[16] The real significance of the causing or permitting offence is that it was held in *Monk v Warbey*[17] to amount to a breach of statutory duty, so that if the victim was unable to recover from the driver, the victim had an additional civil action against the owner: this is no longer relevant as far as the victim is concerned, for the victim of an uninsured driver has a default action against the Motor Insurers Bureau,[18] although the MIB might itself take advantage of subrogation rights[19] to pursue the action against the owner having indemnified the victim.

The UK has taken up to a limited extent the derogation provided for by art 4 of Directive 72/166. Various forms of public service vehicles are, under s 144 of the 1988 Act, excluded from the compulsory insurance requirement, as is a vehicle owned by a person who has made a public deposit of the sum of £500,000.[20]

The Directives do not limit their scope to accidents occurring in

---

13. *(continued)* Uninsured Drivers Agreement, discussed at p 68, below. The cases demonstrate that a passenger who is passive as regards the manner in which the vehicle is being driven is not a user (*Brown v Roberts* [1963] 2 All ER 263; *Hatton v Hall, The Times*, 15 May 1996), whereas a passenger who participates in driving, e.g., by encouraging the driver to speed, is himself a user (*Stinton v Stinton* [1995] RTR 157). The distinction is a fine one, and is based on the concept of 'joint enterprise'. The assured who is a passenger is himself a user (*Cobb v Williams* [1973] RTR 113).

14. S 143(3). This would arise where the user has been informed, possibly by the owner who has loaned the car, that the user is covered under the owner's policy.

15. *Peters v General Accident* [1938] 2 All ER 267.

16. See *Ferrymaster v Adams* [1980] RTR 139.

17. [1935] 1 KB 75.    18. See p 68 below.

19. Such rights are not available, as a matter of law, in a death or personal injury case.

20. The sum deposited is to be used to discharge liabilities which would have been covered by a compulsory policy: Road Traffic Act 1988, s 155 as supplemented by the Motor Vehicles (Third Party Risks) Deposits Regulations 1992, SI 1992 No 1284.

public places, and refer instead to liabilities incurred in the territories of member states. By contrast, the 1988 Act limits the scope of compulsory cover to a 'road', the definition of which in s 192 of the 1988 Act refers to any road to which the public has access. Decisions on the definition have made it clear that private land is excluded unless the public has free access to it,[21] and also that a road must have defined borders and must provide access from one fixed point to another, so that a beach is not a road.[22] If an accident occurs while a vehicle is straddling private land and a road as so defined, the question is whether the vehicle is mainly on private land or on the road.[23] It might be commented that there is nothing in the Directives which justifies the UK's restriction of compulsory cover to public roads.

As far as the term 'vehicle' is concerned, Directive 72/166, art 1(1) provides that a vehicle is 'any motor vehicle intended for travel on land and propelled by mechanical power, but not running on rails, and any trailer, whether or not coupled'. The implementing definition of 'vehicle' in s 185 of the 1988 Act refers to 'a mechanically propelled vehicle intended or adapted for use on roads' and trailers are also within the scope of the Act.[24] There are decisions which indicate that a vehicle which is used on a public road, but which is not intended or adapted for such use – such as a go-kart or racing car – need not be insured.[25] Once again, there is no authority in the Directives for the restriction of compulsory insurance to vehicles intended or designed for use on roads.

UK law cannot, by contrast, be faulted in its provisions on the scope of a compulsory policy. Section 145 requires compulsory cover for the following forms of loss caused by or arising out[26] of the use of a vehicle.

---

[21.] See, e.g., *O'Brien v Trafalgar Insurance* (1945) 78 Ll LR 223; *Buchanan v Motor Insurers Bureau* [1954] 1 Lloyd's Rep 519.

[22.] *McGurk & Dale v Coster* [1995] CL para 2912.

[23.] *Randall v Motor Insurers Bureau* [1969] 1 All ER 1.

[24.] Road Traffic Act 1988, s 145(3).

[25.] See *Burns v Currell* [1963] 2 QB 433; *Brown v Abbott* (1965) 109 SJ 437. The leading authority on the general question is *Chief Constable of Avon and Somerset v Fleming* [1987] 1 All ER 318.

[26.] Directive 76/277 refers to losses 'caused' by motor vehicles, as opposed to losses arising out of their use. The UK formulation is wider: it was thus held in *Dunthorne v Bentley, The Times*, 11 March 1996 that a loss could arise out of the use of the vehicle even where the assured was temporarily outside the vehicle and crossing a road in order to obtain assistance after running out of petrol.

(a) Death or personal injury, to an unlimited amount[27] – the minimum per victim derogation permitted by the Directives has not been adopted. A motor policy is not required to cover liability for the death of, or personal injury to, an employee of the assured, as such liability is insured under the Employers' Liability (Compulsory Insurance) Act 1969, although if the victim employee was using the vehicle at the time the motor policy is to provide cover unless the employers' liability policy itself provides the necessary cover.[28]

(b) Property damage, for a minimum figure of £250,000 and without any deductible as authorised by the derogation in the Directives. Excluded is damage to the vehicle itself, which is a first party risk, and also liability for damage to the property of third parties carried for hire or reward in the vehicle or to any property in the assured's custody or control.[29] Bailment and contractual liabilities are treated by the Act as goods in transit rather than motor risks, and as not falling within the scope of a compulsory motor policy. While this view has much to commend it, the basis of it within the Directives is far from clear.

## Terms of policies

### Scheme of the Directives

The Directives are silent on the precise risks which are to be covered by a compulsory policy, and there is simply a statement in art 3 of Directive 72/166 that the terms and conditions of compulsory insurance are to be determined by member states in implementing the general principle that civil liability in respect of the use of vehicles is to be covered by compulsory insurance. This wording raises the question whether a compulsory policy is to be absolute in its coverage as regards third party victims, or whether it is possible for policies to contain terms which limit the insurer's liability in particular circumstances, e.g., deliberate running down, drunken driving, or failure to maintain a vehicle in an appropriate condition.

---

27. Including a sum for hospital and emergency treatment: Road Traffic Act 1988, ss 157–60 and the Road Traffic Accidents (Payment for Treatment) Order 1993, SI 1993 No 2474, which sets out the required amounts.

28. Road Traffic Act 1988, s 145(4)(a), (4A).

29. Road Traffic Act 1988, s 145(3)(a), (4)(b)–(f).

This question was considered by the European Court of Justice in *Bernáldez*.[30] Spanish law provided that a compulsory motor policy was to exclude liability for property damage caused by an intoxicated driver, and the policy in question so stated. B caused a motor accident in the course of driving while intoxicated, and property damage was sustained by a third party. The European Court of Justice held that Spanish law was incompatible with art 3 of Directive 72/166. The Court laid down the general principle that the article 'precludes an insurer from being able to rely on statutory provisions or contractual clauses to refuse to compensate third party victims of an accident caused by the insured vehicle'. Applying that general principle, the Court further ruled that the exclusion for intoxicated drivers was not permissible.

There are, however, limits to this decision, stemming from the fact that the Directives do not prevent an insurer from adopting exclusion clauses in its policies, but merely prevent their enforcement in so far as the assured's claim is in respect of third party liability within the scope of the Directives. Such a clause is, therefore, operative as regards first party damage and as regards any third party damage beyond the financial limits of compulsory insurance. If the insurer finds itself in the position of having to indemnify the assured for third party losses in circumstances where an otherwise applicable contractual exclusion has been negatived by the law, *Bernáldez* states that domestic law may confer upon the insurer a right of recourse against the assured. This approach has the effect of ensuring that the third party is protected, and that the assured is ultimately at risk for driving in a fashion prohibited by the policy, although it is the insurer rather than the victim who bears the risk of the assured's insolvency.

## UK reception

The Directives are silent as to the formalities which are necessary to bring the cover into existence. The 1988 Act states that the issue of a full policy is not required, and that a cover note will suffice,[31] but it also states, in s 147, that the insurance is not to be effective until the insurer has delivered a certificate of insurance to the assured in the form prescribed under the Act.[32] The purpose of the

---

30. Case C-129/94 [1996] All ER (EC) 741.
31. This follows from the definition of insurance policy in s 161.
32. The prescribed form is laid down by the Motor Vehicles (Third Party Risks) Regulations 1972, 51 1972 No 1217, as amended.

certificate is to act as evidence of the terms of the policy, particularly where the assured is required to produce details of insurance following an accident[33] or on a request by the police. On a strict reading of the Act, the absence of a certificate – for whatever reason – prevents any claim on the policy even though the policy itself is otherwise validly made. That possibility was removed by the Privy Council in *Motor & General Insurance v Cox*,[34] a decision which means that as long as a certificate is issued by the date of any judgment against the assured (the assured being entitled to a certificate) a claim can be made by the assured against the insurers.

It has been noted above that the Directives, as interpreted in *Bernáldez*, require the coverage of compulsory policies to be absolute as far as the third party is concerned. The 1988 Act may not fully comply with this requirement. Section 148 prevents the insurer from relying, in relation to a third party claim as opposed to a first party claim, upon policy terms which govern:[35]

(a) the age or physical or mental condition of persons driving the vehicle;
(b) the condition of the vehicle;
(c) the number of persons that the vehicle carries;
(d) the weight or physical characteristics of the goods that the vehicle carries;
(e) the time at which or the areas within which the vehicle is used;
(f) the horsepower or cylinder capacity or value of the vehicle;
(g) the carrying on the vehicle of any particular apparatus; or
(h) the carrying on the vehicle of any particular means of identification other than any means of identification required to be carried by or under the Vehicles Excise and Registration Act 1994.

This list is not fully exhaustive of the exclusions which may be found in motor insurance contracts. There is, perhaps most importantly, a common restriction confining the use of the vehicle to social, domestic or pleasure purposes, or possibly to non-business purposes,[36] and it is far from clear that this restriction can be fitted in to any of the matters set out above. The

---

33. See p 68 below.  34. [1990] 1 WLR 1443.  35. S 148(2).
36. Note, however, that s 151 of the 1988 Act provides that car sharing arrangements for lifts to work are to be regarded as a social, domestic or pleasure use of the vehicle for the purposes of a compulsory insurance policy.

effect of *Bernáldez* would seem to be that all exclusion clauses are ineffective as against a third party. *Bernáldez* may well have the effect of negativing the common law rule that deliberate misconduct – e.g., running down – prevents a claim by the assured (and thereby denies any possibility of recovery to the victim) as a matter of public policy and independently of the policy wording.[37] However, it should be said that the English courts have refused to extend that rule to motor policies, and that loss caused by the assured's deliberate conduct is to be treated as insured.[38] UK law takes advantage of the possibility left open by *Bernáldez* that, in the event that an insurer is required to meet a third party claim despite the fact that it would have been excluded by the policy, the insurer has a right of recourse against the assured.[39]

The 1988 Act further prevents the insurer from relying upon contractual defences which have arisen after the event giving rise to a claim, e.g., failure to claim within the time laid down by the contract or admission of liability. Such defences are not available as regards third party liability.[40]

### Other defences open to insurers

The Directives operate on the assumption that, if there is a policy in force, the insurer is liable under it, irrespective of the policy's express terms, and the 1988 Act – with minor exceptions which are probably unenforceable under EC law – conforms to that principle. The Directives do not address the possibility that the insurer has the right to avoid the policy for the assured's pre-contractual misrepresentations or failure to disclose material facts, and it is to be assumed that in such a case the Directives leave the insurer's rights unaffected. Accordingly, if the policy is avoided, the assured is to be treated as uninsured and the victim must look to the Motor Insurers Bureau for the sums due from the driver.

UK law seeks to cast the burden back on to the original insurer. Section 152(2) of the 1988 Act maintains the insurer's defence, but

---

37. As in *Gray v Barr* [1971] 2 QB 544.
38. *Tinline v White Cross Insurance* [1921] 3 KB 327; *James v British General Insurance* [1927] 2 KB 311, both motor insurance cases predating the introduction of compulsory cover; *Hardy v Motor Insurers Bureau* [1964] 2 QB 745; *Gardner v Moore* [1984] 1 All ER 1100, both cases being claims against the MIB rather than the assured's own insurers.
39. Road Traffic Act 1988, s 148(4).     40. Road Traffic Act 1988, s 148(5).

provides that it cannot be relied upon unless the insurer has, within three months from the date on which the victim's action against the driver was commenced, itself commenced proceedings for injunctive or declaratory relief. If the time limit is missed by the insurer, the defence is lost as far as the third party's claim is concerned. The insurer is entitled to be informed by the victim of the commencement of proceedings against the driver, either before or within seven days of such commencement, so that the insurer's right to seek relief within three months is not prejudiced by lack of information.[41]

## Drivers covered by policy

### Scheme of the Directives

Directive 72/166 in its original form required a compulsory policy to cover only the driver of the vehicle. A major extension was made by art 2(1) of Directive 85/2. Under this provision, any term in a compulsory policy is void in so far as it seeks to exclude liability for accidents caused by any of the following persons.

(a) A person who does not have express or implied authorisation to drive. The purpose is, therefore, to ensure that the insurer is liable not just for the insured driver, but also for any other person driving the vehicle, whether a person who has borrowed the vehicle with the assured's consent or whether a thief. The effect is, therefore, to convert a motor insurer from an insurer of the named assured into an insurer of the vehicle itself, irrespective of who happened to be behind the wheel at the time. Member states are, by way of derogation, entitled to allow insurers to enforce a clause excluding liability for unauthorised driving as against a person injured after voluntarily entering the vehicle knowing that it had been stolen. By way of further derogation, member states are given the option of allowing an insurer to deny liability for losses caused by a thief, provided that such losses are recoverable from the national Motor Insurers Bureau.

(b) A person not licensed to drive the vehicle. The Directive requires the insurer to accept liability even for a person who is not permitted by law to drive a vehicle by reason of not being

---

41. Under Road Traffic Act 1988, s 152(2), discussed below.

licensed to do so. Combining (a) and (b), it will be seen that the theft of a vehicle by an unlicensed (perhaps, underage) person can result in the insurer facing liability for accidents caused by the driver.

(c) A person driving the vehicle in breach of safety requirements laid down by domestic law.

Article 2(1) provides that these extensions to a policy can be removed where a member state's social security rules make compensation available in place of insurance.

### UK reception

Prior to the adoption of the Directives, it had been the position in the UK that any person identified in the policy – whether by name or by class, e.g., any person authorised by the assured – as entitled to drive, was regarded as having a direct right against the insurer under the policy.[42] The general position remained, however, that the insurer was liable only to the assured or to a person covered by the policy. The extension of the law to coverage for unauthorised drivers, and thereby the focus of the policy from the assured to the car, was achieved by amendments introduced in 1987 and which now constitute s 151 of the Road Traffic Act 1988. The general effect of s 151(2) is to require the insurer to cover the liability both of any insured driver, and of any other driver other than in respect of a passenger who knew or ought to have been aware that the vehicle had been stolen or unlawfully taken.[43] An insurer faced with such extended liability, has a right of recourse against the unauthorised driver or against the assured if the latter has allowed the vehicle to be driven by a person not covered by the express terms of the policy.[44]

## Victims

### Scheme of the Directives

Directive 72/166 required insurance to be in place for all victims of road accidents. This general requirement was amplified by two

---

[42.] Now Road Traffic Act 1988, s 148(7).
[43.] Road Traffic Act 1988, s 151(4) – p 66, below.
[44.] Road Traffic Act 1988, s 151(7), (8).

subsequent amendments. Article 3 of Directive 84/5 provides that the members of the family of the insured person, driver or other person facing liability under the civil law for injury are not to be excluded from insurance in respect of their personal injuries. Further, art 1 of Directive 90/232 states that passengers in the vehicle, other than the driver, are to be protected by compulsory insurance. The protection of passengers is, however, restricted by art 2(1) of Directive 84/5, which, it will be recalled, allows member states to deny a passenger the benefit of insurance where the passenger is injured in a vehicle which, to the passenger's knowledge, had been stolen. The position under EC law is therefore that a compulsory policy: (a) need not cover the driver; (b) must cover passengers other than those driving in a stolen vehicle; and (c) must cover members of the assured's family as if they were arm's length third parties.

*UK reception*

UK law has never distinguished between members of the assured's family and third parties, and the 1988 Act makes no mention of them. The position of the driver of a vehicle and of passengers is rather more complex.

Turning first to the driver, whether or not the driver is covered is a matter for the determination of member states, as art 1 of Directive 90/232 specifically states that the driver is not required to be protected. In the UK it was held, prior to the 1987 amendments, in *Cooper v Motor Insurers Bureau*,[45] that the driver is excluded from the Act, and accordingly from a policy which does no more than offer compulsory cover. It was subsequently asserted in *R v Secretary of State for Transport, Ex parte National Insurance Guarantee Corporation*,[46] that the 1988 Act was to be construed, in accordance with EC law, as extending compulsory cover to drivers. The Court of Appeal rejected this argument, holding that both the Act and the Directives were clear in excluding the driver. If the assured is a passenger in the vehicle, the Act would appear to cover the assured in the same way as any other passenger.[47]

---

[45] [1985] 1 All ER 449.
[46] *The Times*, 3 June 1996.
[47] *Limbrick v French and Farley* [1990] CLY 2709. Standard policy wording probably leads to the same result: *Digby v General Accident* [1943] AC 121.

As far as passengers are concerned, the 1988 Act extends liability cover to injuries suffered by passengers in the same way as external third parties, although earlier versions of the legislation had confined such protection to passengers who were not being carried for hire or reward. The derogation for passengers in stolen cars has been taken up by the UK: s 151(4) denies an action against the insurer to a person who has suffered injury or property damage if, at the time of that damage, that person was being carried in or on a vehicle which they knew *or had reason to believe* had been stolen or unlawfully taken. The italicised words are not justified by the Directives, and it is arguable that a person who was unaware of the theft but ought to have been is nevertheless entitled under the Directives to the benefit of any insurance attaching to the vehicle.

It is to be noted that, as regards passengers, the Directives are concerned only with the ambit of the policy, and not with the civil law which confers upon the passenger rights against the driver which trigger the policy. It might be thought that if the civil law does not confer the necessary cause of action against negligent drivers, there is little point in having insurance in place. While the Directives do not address this matter, UK law does, to a limited extent. Section 149 of the 1988 Act outlaws two possible defences which a driver might have to a civil claim by a passenger: any agreement between the driver and the passenger restricting the driver's liability is of no effect; and a driver may not plead the defence of *volenti non fit injuria* against a passenger, e.g., where the passenger has voluntarily accepted a lift with a drunken driver or where the driver has warned the passenger that the driver accepts no liability for injuries caused. However, the Act leaves untouched two other common law defences which may restrict or defeat the passenger's civil rights: a plea of contributory negligence as regards a passenger who has partly caused their own injuries, e.g., by not wearing a seat belt or crash helmet;[48] and a plea of public policy where the passenger has participated in (as opposed to having been present at) unlawful conduct by the driver, which may consist of dangerous driving[49] or some extraneous illegality which the car is being used to further.[50]

---

48. See *Froom v Butcher* [1976] QB 286, which indicated that a deduction of up to 20% is appropriate in many such cases.
49. *Pitts v Hunt* [1990] 3 All ER 344.
50. *Ashton v Turner* [1981] 1 QB 137.

## The victim's claim

### Ensuring payment to the victim

The victim's claim is necessarily against the assured, on the basis of the assured's civil liability.[51] The Directives operate on the assumption that, if the victim obtains judgment against the assured, the insurer will indemnify the assured who will in turn pay the insurance moneys to the victim. Two problems may here arise. The first is that the assured may, having received the insurance moneys, become insolvent. At common law, the insurance moneys merge into the assured's general assets, so that they become available for distribution to all of the assured's creditors and not just the victim for whom they are earmarked. The Directives do not make any provision for this possibility.

The second, and consequential, problem is that the assured will almost certainly become insolvent when the judgment against the assured is given, and again as a matter of common law the sums payable by the insurer form part of the assured's general assets for distribution to all creditors. EC law does not attempt to resolve this problem, and leaves it to the domestic law of each member state to secure payment to the victim rather than to the assured's other creditors. The UK's approach in s 151 of the 1988 Act is to confer upon the victim a direct claim against the insurer on obtaining judgment against the assured. This prevents any payment to the assured, and ensures that the sums are earmarked for the victim.

### Formalities

The Directives leave to domestic law the manner in which the victim is to receive the benefits of the driver's compulsory insurance. In the UK, as discussed above, the victim is given a direct action against the insurer. That action is, however, subject to the important precondition that the victim must, before or within seven days of commencing proceedings against the assured, notify the insurer of those proceedings.[52] There are numerous authorities on the amount of information which has to be given,

---

51. Such liability is, by the Road Traffic Act 1988, s 153, preserved despite the assured's insolvency.
52. Road Traffic Act 1988, s 152(1).

their general effect being that the information must be specific and must state clearly that proceedings are to be or have been commenced,[53] and not merely that solicitors have advised the victim to commence proceedings.[54] The importance of the notice condition has, however, been weakened by a Scottish decision, *McBlain v Dolan*,[55] which apparently holds that an insurer cannot rely upon the absence of notice if it was independently aware of the claim, and that in any event if the insurer does not have any ground for seeking to avoid the policy for misrepresentation or non-disclosure – which is the primary purpose for requiring notice to be given[56] – the absence of notice is no defence.

## Information

Article 5 of Directive 90/232 imposes an obligation on member states to ensure that the parties involved in a motor accident are able to ascertain promptly the identity of the insurer covering any liability arising out of the accident. UK legislation had previously so provided. Under what is now s 154 of the Road Traffic Act 1988, a person against whom a claim is made must, on demand, state whether he or she is insured and, if so, provide the insurance details set out in the certificate of insurance. It is an offence for the driver not to comply with these obligations.

## Default provision where no insurance exists

### Motor Insurers Bureau

The purpose of compulsory liability insurance is to ensure that the victims of road traffic accidents have a fund against which a claim may be made in order to compensate them for their injuries. However, the purpose breaks down in two situations: where the driver is uninsured and does not have sufficient resources to meet the victim's claim, and where the victim is a sufferer of a 'hit and run' accident, so that the identity of the driver (and thus of the insurance company) cannot be ascertained. These lacunae in the

---

[53]. *Ceylon Motor Insurance Association v Thambugala* [1953] AC 584; *McGoona v Motor Insurers Bureau* [1969] 2 Lloyd's Rep 34.
[54]. *Harrington v Link Motor Policies* [1989] 2 Lloyd's Rep 310.
[55]. *The Times*, 28 September 1995.
[56]. See above, p 63, discussing s 152(2) of the 1988 Act.

compulsory insurance scheme were recognised and dealt with in 1946. In that year, motor insurers formed the Motor Insurers Bureau, which in the same year entered into two agreements with the government, the Uninsured Drivers Agreement and the Untraced Drivers Agreement. The general effect of the Agreements was that the MIB would accept liability in the case of injuries caused by an uninsured and insolvent driver, or an untraced driver. The agreements were updated in 1972. A new Uninsured Drivers Agreement was entered into in 1987, following the changes to the law consequent upon the implementation of the Directives, but the Untraced Drivers Agreement of 1972 remains in place, unamended. The Agreements remain non-statutory, and as a matter of law are unenforceable by a victim, as the victim has no privity of contract with the MIB, but it is quite clear that the courts will not permit any such defence to be taken by the MIB.[57]

## The Directives

The scheme adopted in the UK for providing fallback protection was adopted by the EC in Directive 84/5. Article 1(4) of that Directive requires member states to establish a body with the task of providing compensation for personal injury and property damage caused by uninsured and untraced drivers. Member states are empowered to confer upon the body (which may be called for convenience a Motor Insurers Bureau) so established a right of recourse against the driver and against other insurers or social security providers, but the point was that the Motor Insurers Bureau is to be primarily responsible to the victim. This point was emphasised by an amendment to art 1(4) by art 3 of Directive 90/232, under which the Motor Insurers Bureau charged with liability for meeting uninsured losses or losses caused by an untraced driver cannot make payment conditional on the victim proving that the driver is unable to pay. Article 4 of Directive 90/232, recognising that in some cases it may be unclear whether the victim's injury or loss is covered by an insurance policy or by the Motor Insurers Bureau (e.g., where the validity of the policy is in question), provides that each member state must make either the insurer or the Motor Insurers Bureau primarily liable to the victim – so that the victim's compensation is not delayed by any such

---

57. *Gurtner v Circuit* [1968] 2 QB 587.

dispute – and that the matter is to be resolved as between the insurer and the bureau at a later date.

Article 1(4) does not require member states to provide, through the Motor Insurers Bureau established by them, exhaustive coverage of losses which must be protected by compulsory insurance. Three important derogations are permitted:

(a) all property damage caused by untraced (but not uninsured) drivers;
(b) property damage caused by uninsured drivers below the amount of 500 ecu;
(c) compensation for bodily injury suffered by a person who voluntarily entered the vehicle knowing that it was uninsured.

The existence of a fallback compensation body led to the suggestion in *Bernáldez*[58] that it was permissible for an insurer to exclude liability in specific circumstances, as a victim of a driver whose policy did not cover the loss in question would in those circumstances have a direct cause of action against the motor insurers bureau. The European Court of Justice held that the Directives do not permit an insurer to cast the burden of liability on the Motor Insurers Bureau, and that the position was that such policy provisions were void in respect of third party claims.

### Uninsured drivers

The MIB Uninsured Drivers Agreement of 1987 provides compensation to the victim of a driver who either has no policy at all, or whose policy is no longer valid. It is necessary for the victim to prove that the compulsory insurance requirement attached to the circumstances in which the vehicle was being used. The MIB then faces the statutory liabilities of unlimited sums for death and personal injury, and £250,000 for property damage: the Agreement, in accordance with the derogation in Directive 90/232, art 1(4), requires the victim to bear the first £175 of property damage (a restriction which does not exist where there is insurance in place). The Agreement also takes advantage of the derogation in Directive 90/232 in respect of a person who voluntarily entered the vehicle knowing that it was uninsured, and adopts also the

---

58. Case C-129/94 [1996] All ER (EC) 741.

derogation in Directive 84/5, art 2, in respect of a person who voluntarily entered the vehicle knowing that it was stolen: to this end, the Agreement provides that a person suffering bodily injury cannot recover from the MIB if that person was voluntarily in or on the vehicle and knew *or ought to have known* that the vehicle was uninsured or stolen. It has been pointed out above that the Directives refer only to actual knowledge, and not to knowledge which the victim ought to have had, and that the italicised words are probably unenforceable. The point is important, for in *Hadfield v Knowles*[59] it was held that those words laid down a combined objective and subjective test, so that where the victim was aware that the driver was disqualified, but did not appreciate that he was necessarily thereby uninsured, she was unable to recover from the MIB: her actual (subjective) knowledge was to be treated as if it were in the possession of a reasonable person (objective), and a reasonable person would have appreciated that the driver was uninsured. It is thought that this decision cannot stand with the wording of the Directives.

*Untraced drivers*

The Untraced Drivers Agreement of 1972 is largely taken up with the problem that, in the case of a hit and run accident, there may be no evidence as to the circumstances and thus of whether there was any negligence on the part of the driver. The Agreement accordingly provides for investigation of the accident coupled with arbitration in the event of any dispute. The most important feature of the Agreement is that it follows the derogation in Directive 90/232 in respect of property damage, and confers a right of recovery on the victim of an untraced driver in respect of bodily injury only.

# The Single Market for compulsory motor insurance

The first two generations of Non-Life Insurance Directives, Directives 73/239 and 88/357, created, as will be recalled from chapter 1, a system whereby an insurer authorised and established in any one member state was entitled to become established in

59. 1993, unreported.

another, host, member state or to sell large risks insurance into a host state. Motor vehicle insurance was excluded from this scheme pending harmonisation of substantive requirements. The two earlier Directives were subsequently amended by Directive 90/618,[60] rectifying the omission of motor insurance. The Third Non-Life Directive, Directive 92/49, which completed the Single Market by abolishing the distinction between large risks and mass risks, applied also to motor vehicle insurance.

The result of the Directives, as amended, is that a motor insurer established and authorised in a member state is entitled to become established in a host state or to sell motor insurance by way of services into a host state. Two additional requirements are imposed. First, the insurer must join the national Motor Insurers Bureau of the host state. Secondly, in the case of an insurer selling into the host state from an establishment in another member state, the insurer must appoint a claims representative in the host state; this requirement is intended to ensure that a policyholder or claimant against a policyholder has a point of contact with the insurer within the host state.

These provisions were originally implemented in the UK by statutory instrument in 1992[61] by way of amendment to the primary legislation. A compulsory policy is, under s 145(2), (5), (6) of the Road Traffic Act 1988, valid only if it is issued by an authorised insurer or an insurer entitled to provide motor insurance in the UK under EC rules, in either case being a member of the Motor Insurers Bureau. The Insurance Companies Act 1982, Sched 2G, para 11, repeats that an EC company is entitled to provide insurance in the UK only if it is a member of the MIB and, in the case of the provision of insurance by way of services, if it has appointed a claims representative for the UK. A claims representative fulfils the requirements of the 1982 Act if:[62]

(a) authorised to act on behalf of the insurer in relation to any matters giving rise to claims, to pay sums in settlement of claims and to accept service of proceedings on behalf of the insurer;

(b) authorised to represent the insurer in any proceedings to establish the existence or validity of a policy issued by the insurer;

60. Inserting art 12a into Directive 88/357.
61. The Motor Vehicles (Compulsory Insurance) Regulations 1992, SI 1992 No 3036.
62. Insurance Companies Act 1982, s 96F.

(c) their authority is limited to motor business;
(d) resident in the host state (or, in the case of a company, has a place of business in the host state).

# CHAPTER FOUR

# Insurance intermediaries

## General principles of agency law

### Authority of agents

Any act of an agent binds his principal if it falls within the scope of the agent's authority. An agent's authority may be established under one of four headings.

(1) *Actual authority*, consisting of the express instructions given to the agent, plus any authority which must necessarily be implied in order to fulfil express instructions. It is not necessary for the agent to disclose that he or she is acting on behalf of a principal, the rule being that as long as the agent is authorised to act on behalf of the principal and intends to do so the principal is bound by the agent's act. An agent with instructions to insure may, therefore, create a contract of insurance between the assured and a third party (the insurer) even though the contract is made in the agent's own name.[1]

(2) *Usual authority*, consisting of the authority which an agent of the type in question would normally be expected to have. If the principal imposes any limitations on the usual authority of the agent, those limitations must be brought to the attention of the person with whom the agent is dealing, as otherwise that person is entitled to assume that there are no limitations.

[1.] *National Oilwell v Davy Offshore* [1993] 2 Lloyd's Rep 582, where the requisite intention was absent; *Siu v Eastern Insurance Ltd* [1994] 2 AC 199. The difficulty here is in reconciling the undisclosed principal rule with the insurance rule that all material facts must be disclosed to the insurer. These cases are discussed in FMB Reynolds, 'Some Agency Problems in Insurance Law', in Rose (ed), *Consensus Ad Idem* (Sweet & Maxwell, 1996), pp 77–95. The agent may, in addition, be personally liable on a contract of this type as the agent may be regarded as a party to the contract.

(3) *Apparent authority*, consisting of authority which would not normally be possessed by an agent of the type in question but which the principal has indicated – by word or deed – that the agent does indeed possess. Apparent authority, also known as agency by estoppel, operates to prevent the insurer from denying the impression which it has given to the other party. As what is involved is a personal estoppel against the principal, it follows that the agent cannot, by an assertion of authority, bind the principal unless the principal has in some way associated himself or herself with that assertion.[2]

(4) *Ratification*, which arises where an agent who has not been authorised to perform a particular act on the part of the principal nevertheless does so, and where the principal subsequently adopts the agent's act. It is necessary for the agent to have acted in the principal's name, as an undisclosed principal is not permitted to ratify an unauthorised act.[3] In the insurance context, if the agent has procured insurance in the assured's name without the assured's authority, the assured is seemingly entitled to ratify even though aware that a loss has occurred.[4]

The fact that an agent has acted fraudulently does not alter the above principles, as the only question is whether, from the third party's point of view, the agent has acted within the scope of their authority.[5] If, however, the agent has acted outside the scope of their authority, so that the principal is not bound by the agent's acts, the third party may bring personal proceedings against the agent for breach of warranty of authority.[6]

### Duties of the parties

The agent's duty is to exercise reasonable care in obeying instructions given by the principal. An important aspect of this

---

2. See generally, *First Energy v Hungarian International Bank* [1993] 2 Lloyd's Rep 194.
3. *Keighley, Maxsted v Durant* [1901] AC 240.
4. This is clearly the case in marine insurance under the Marine Insurance Act 1906, s 86, and while there is old authority for the proposition that ratification is not possible at this stage (*Williams v North China Insurance* (1876) 1 CPD 757), the modern view is that the more generous marine rule should apply in all cases: *National Oilwell v Davy Offshore* [1993] 2 Lloyd's Rep 582.
5. *Lloyd v Grace Smith* [1912] AC 716.    6. *Yonge v Toynbee* [1910] 1 KB 215.

duty is that the agent must not put himself or herself in a position in which duty to the principal conflicts with the agent's own interest[7] or in which the agent undertakes duties to the third party and is unable fully to further the principal's interests: the courts are unlikely to imply any duty of care on an agent towards the third party if this would result in the creation of a possible conflict between that duty and the agent's duty to the principal.[8]

In return, the principal is required to remunerate the agent, either on the agreed basis – commonly commission – or on a *quantum meruit* basis in the absence of express agreement. The principal is also required to indemnify the agent for any expenditure incurred by the agent in the course of performing their duties. There is no statutory code of mutual rights and duties for agents selling services – including insurance – on behalf of their principals, but there is such a code for agents selling goods on behalf of their principals. This is found in the Commercial Agents (Council Directive) Regulations 1993,[9] which implement the EC Directive on Commercial Agents.[10] The Directive and the implementing Regulations contain complex and controversial rules on the termination of the agency relationship and the entitlement of the agent to compensation for loss of future commission whether the contract has been terminated lawfully or not.[11] As will be seen below, the extension of the Directive to services would have caused particular difficulty in the context of insurance, as the general rule applicable to insurance brokers is that commission is paid not by the broker's principal, the assured, but rather by the insurer.

# Intermediaries in the insurance market

## Agents of insurers

An insurance intermediary, defined in the broadest terms, is any person who acts for either the insurer or the assured in the course of negotiations and in the administration of the contract.

---

7. An agent may not, therefore, make secret profits out of the agency.
8. See *White v Jones* [1995] 1 All ER 691, per Lord Browne-Wilkinson at p 718. For the operation of this principle as regards insurance brokers, see p 80 below.
9. SI 1993 No 3053.    10. 86/653/EC.
11. For discussion, see FMB Reynolds [1994] JBL 265–270.

Inevitably, a large number of intermediaries may be involved. Leaving aside the fact that a corporate insurer or assured can as a legal person act only through its employees and agents, it is possible to identify a number of persons who are not employees of either party but who act as intermediaries. On the insurer's side, the most important classes of agent are as follows.

## Marketing agents

Insurers in practice operate to a large extent through commission agents, whose function is to obtain proposals from potential assureds for consideration by insurers. Such agents do not normally have authority to grant temporary or full cover, unless some form of estoppel against the insurer can be established, and the insurer will otherwise be bound by all of the agent's acts within the scope of the agent's authority.[12]

## Underwriting agents[13]

Insurers frequently delegate authority to accept risks to third parties. At Lloyd's, it is common to find that an underwriter has been granted authority by other underwriters to subscribe to specific risks,[14] and brokers may be granted 'binding authorities' (usually referred to as 'binders') by Lloyd's underwriters and insurers under which risks can be accepted for the subscribing insurers. A further mechanism, which became increasingly popular in the 1970s, but which in recent years has been characterised by spectacular insolvencies, is the use of an underwriting agent. This type of agent has delegated to it by one or more insurers (or, more commonly in practice, reinsurers) the authority to enter contracts on behalf of those insurers. Underwriting agents will also be

---

12. See below. This is subject to the curious rule, confirmed by the Court of Appeal in *Newsholme Brothers v Road Transport and General Insurance* [1929] 2 KB 256, that where the agent completes the proposal form on behalf of the assured the agent does so as the assured's amanuensis, so that material facts in the agent's possession which are not passed on to the insurer may be relied upon by the insurer to avoid the policy for non-disclosure. The rule is anomalous and probably cannot withstand analysis: see *Stone v Reliance Mutual* [1972] 1 Lloyd's Rep 469.
13. Agents of investors at Lloyd's – members' agents and managing agents – are also collectively referred to as 'underwriting agents', but their functions are rather different. See below, p 82.
14. Such an authority is referred to as a 'line slip'.

empowered to receive premiums and to pay losses, on behalf of insurers.

The use of underwriting agents has in the past been seen in part as a convenient method of avoiding regulatory requirements. The assumed legal structure has been that the underwriting agent operates in the UK and accepts risks in the UK on behalf of the participating insurers, while the participating insurers are located offshore: as the underwriting agent is not an insurer, it does not require authorisation, and as the insurers are located offshore, they do not carry on insurance business in the UK, with the result that no UK authorisations are required. A recent decision of the Court of Appeal, *Re Great Western Insurance Ltd*,[15] has denied that the regulatory requirements can be evaded in this way: the Court ruled that a participating insurer does carry on business in the UK, by reason of having authorised the underwriting agent to act on its behalf in the UK, and accordingly must be authorised. The Court confirmed, however, that the underwriting agent does not require authorisation, as the agent does not bear the risks associated with insurance activity.

### Local agents

Most insurers operate through local agents and branch offices. Ordinary agency rules apply to local agents: the insurer is bound if there is authority or ratification of unauthorised acts, but not otherwise. If the policy or other documentation given to the assured provides that certain matters have to be dealt with by head office alone, the assured cannot rely upon the usual authority of an agent.[16] By contrast, if the insurer has provided the indicia of authority, e.g., by allowing the agent to have possession of blank cover notes, the assured can rely upon an estoppel against the insurer.[17]

### Loss adjusters

Loss adjusters are agents appointed by insurers to investigate the circumstances, and to determine the amount, of any loss. Their duties are owed exclusively to insurers, and their competence is

---

[15.] 1996, unreported
[16.] Of the many illustrations, see *Acey v Fernie* (1840) 7 M & W 153.
[17.] *Murfitt v Royal Insurance* (1922) 38 TLR 334 is a representative decision.

regulated by the professional bodies to which they belong. The EC Recommendation on Intermediaries (see below) apparently has no application to this sector.

## Establishments: branches and agencies

An insurer wishing to offer insurance in a member state other than its home state of establishment and authorisation may do so, under the Single European Licence, either by becoming established in the host state or by selling insurance by way of services into the host state from an establishment in another member state.[18] The distinction between establishment and services is significant for regulatory purposes, as the formal requirements for establishment are less onerous. An establishment is generally thought of as a subsidiary or branch, but the Second Generation of Insurance Directives provides that any 'permanent presence' is to be treated as an establishment. A permanent presence may be no more than 'an office managed by the undertaking's own staff or by a person who is independent but has permanent authority to act for the undertaking as an agency would'.[19] The question which arises regularly, but which has yet to be given an authoritative answer, is whether a broker operating under a binding authority, or an underwriting agent, is to be regarded as an establishment: if this is the case, the grant of a binding authority to an intermediary will attract the requirements applicable to the creation of an establishment.[20]

## Agents of assureds

### Brokers

An insurance broker is an independent agent, and it has long been the law that, by approaching the broker and instructing him or her to obtain insurance, the assured thereby appoints the broker as their agent.[21] This rule is on occasion somewhat difficult to reconcile with the realities of the broking function, and particularly with the settled role of the broker in drafting policy

---

18. See the general discussion in chapter 1.
19. Second Non-Life Directive, art 3; Second Life Directive, art 3.
20. For further discussion of this problem, see chapter 1.
21. *Roberts v Plaisted* [1989] 2 Lloyd's Rep 341.

wording,[22] acting as coverholder under a binding authority which involves selecting assureds to be declared to the cover offered by the insurer,[23] and obtaining reports for underwriters on the nature and extent of the assured's loss.[24] The courts have resolved the problem by holding that the broker, while primarily the assured's agent, may act for the insurer provided that no conflict of interest arises[25] or that the assured has given free and informed consent,[26] and that it is a question of fact in every case whether the broker is acting for the assured or the insurer.[27]

Perhaps the greatest theoretical difficulty flows from the long-established but anomalous rule that the level of a broker's commission – traditionally deducted by the broker from the assured's premium – is agreed between the insurer and the broker rather than the assured and the broker, and is paid by the insurer to the broker as a reward for obtaining business.[28] General agency law regards as anathema any proposition that an agent may be remunerated by the other party, but insurance law recognises the exception as based on custom or implied term. The independence of the broker is maintained by a suggested, although far from settled, implied common law obligation on the broker to disclose the level of commission at the assured's request, at least where it exceeds market norms.[29] It is uncertain whether the common law

---

22. *Youell v Bland Welch (No 1)* [1992] 2 Lloyd's Rep 127, which decides that, as the drafting is carried out by the assured's agent, in the event of ambiguity the *contra proferentem* principle of construction cannot operate in the assured's favour. In so far as the assured is a consumer, within the Unfair Terms in Consumer Contracts Regulations 1994 implementing the EC Unfair Contract Terms Directive (as to which, see chapter 2), the *contra proferentem* principle is reinstated by reg 4 of the Regulations.

23. The point arose in *Empress Assurance v Bowring* (1905) 11 Com Cas 107, in which it was held that the broker does not owe any duty of care to the insurer in exercising judgment under a binding authority. See, however, *Pryke v Gibbs Hartley Cooper* [1991] 1 Lloyd's Rep 602, where the broker undertook specific duties for the insurer unconnected with any duties to the assured.

24. The courts have condemned this form of conduct for creating a conflict of interest: *North and South Trust v Berkeley* [1971] 1 All ER 980.

25. *General Accident v Tanter, The Zephyr* [1985] 2 Lloyd's Rep 529, where a contractual obligation to reinsurers was imposed upon the broker in circumstances where there was no conflict with his duty to reinsureds.

26. *Excess Life v Fireman's Fund of New Jersey* [1982] 2 Lloyd's Rep 599.

27. *Winter v Irish Life* [1995] 2 Lloyd's Rep 274.

28. *Power v Butcher* (1829) 10 B & C 329; *Workman v London & Lancashire Fire* (1903) 19 TLR 360. On the question of causation, see *McNeil v Steamship Mutual* (1940) 67 Ll LR 142.

29. See e.g., *Baring v Stanton* (1876) 3 Ch D 502; *Green v Tunghan* (1913) 30 TLR 64.

custom as to the payment of commission could survive any EC law requiring the independence of brokers.[30]

The duties of a broker, which are owed concurrently in contract and tort,[31] cover all aspects of the contract. The broker's basic duty is, so far as possible or legal, to obey the assured's instructions and to exercise reasonable care in doing so. Relevant matters include: obtaining a policy of the right type and at the right time,[32] covering the assured's needs;[33] choosing a solvent and authorised insurer;[34] ensuring that the application to the insurer contains all material facts and does not omit material information;[35] providing information on the meaning of the policy and the assured's duties under it;[36] and submitting claims to insurers on behalf of the assured.[37]

In addition to duties owed to the assured, a broker may owe duties to a third party who is sufficiently proximate to the transaction and who might foreseeably be harmed by the broker's negligence, provided of course that there is no conflict between the broker's duty to the assured and the implied duty to the third party. The courts have held that a broker owes a duty of care to an identified assignee of the policy,[38] but not to a person who is only indirectly interested in the policy, such as a general creditor of the assured.[39]

---

30. See p 92 below for discussion of this aspect of the Commission's Recommendation on Intermediaries.

31. By analogy with *Henderson v Merrett Syndicates Ltd* [1994] 3 All ER 506, confirming a line of authority consisting most importantly of *Youell v Bland Welch (No 2)* [1990] 2 Lloyd's Rep 431 and *Punjab National Bank v De Boinville* [1992] 3 All ER 104. The main significance of this is that the extended limitation period in the Limitation Act 1986 applicable to tort claims over contract claims – the so-called 'discoverability' period introduced by the Latent Damage Act 1986 – applies to claims against brokers, and that the Law Reform (Contributory Negligence) Act 1945 allows apportionment whether the assured's action against the broker is framed in contract or tort.

32. See, e.g., *McNealy v Pennine Insurance* [1978] 2 Lloyd's Rep 18; *Jones v Crawley Colosso* (1996) 1 Lloyd's List, 1 August.

33. Which are to be ascertained both from express instructions and from the practice of the market: *O'Brien v Hughes Gibb* [1995] LRLR 90.

34. *Osman v Moss* [1970] 1 Lloyd's Rep 313; *Bates v Robert Barrow Ltd* [1995] 1 Lloyd's Rep 680.

35. *O'Connor v Kirby* [1972] 1 QB 80; *Winter v Irish Life* [1995] 2 Lloyd's Rep 274.

36. *Melik v Norwich Union* [1980] 1 Lloyd's Rep 523.

37. *Grace v Leslie & Godwin Financial Services Ltd* [1995] LRLR 472.

38. *Bromley LBC v Ellis* [1971] 1 Lloyd's Rep 97; *Punjab National Bank v De Boinville* [1992] 3 All ER 104.

39. *Verderame v Commercial Union* [1992] BCLC 793 (shareholder in assured company); *Federation General v Knott Becker* [1990] 1 Lloyd's Rep 98 (victim of assured's negligence).

## Lloyd's agents

Lloyd's brokers are insurance brokers accredited at Lloyd's, the significance of accreditation being that only a Lloyd's broker can seek insurance on the Lloyd's market from underwriters. Other brokers who wish to place insurance at Lloyd's must enter into some form of arrangement with a Lloyd's broker whereby the Lloyd's broker either 'fronts' for the broker or at least acts as sub-agent. The relationship between Lloyd's brokers and underwriters is necessarily very close, as the numbers of each are limited and all dealings take place on a face-to-face basis. Nevertheless, the rule remains that a Lloyd's broker is the agent of the assured rather than the agent of the underwriters with whom insurance is placed, so that facts known to a Lloyd's broker which are not communicated to the underwriters are treated as not having been disclosed.[40]

It should be mentioned, for the sake of completeness, that two other forms of agent operate at Lloyd's, namely, members' agents and managing agents. These agents, collectively referred to as 'underwriting agents' (and not to be confused with underwriting agents used by insurers, discussed earlier), act as agents of investors (names) at Lloyd's. The function of a members' agent is to act as investment adviser to a name, recommending the spread of syndicates which the name should adopt in order to balance the prospects of profit with the risks of loss. The function of a managing agent is to ensure that business underwritten by a Lloyd's syndicate does not unduly expose the names, in terms of the nature and amount of the risks written and the adequacy of reinsurance cover obtained for the names.[41]

## Other agents

A variety of other persons whose main business is the supply of goods or services may act as agents for assureds for the purposes of placing ancillary insurance with an external insurer. Numerous examples exist, the most important categories consisting of banks

---

40. *Roberts v Plaisted* [1989] 2 Lloyd's Rep 341, a rule which caused the Court of Appeal to recommend legislative reform following an investigation by the Law Commission.

41. The relevant principles are set out in *Henderson v Merrett Syndicates Ltd* [1994] 3 All ER 506, *Aiken v Stewart Wrightson Members Agency* [1995] 3 All ER 449 and *Brown v KMR Services Ltd* [1995] 4 All ER 598.

and building societies offering life and property insurance connected with a loan secured by mortgage, travel agents offering holiday cover, sellers of electrical goods offering extended warranty protection and solicitors obtaining cover to protect the interests of the parties to a conveyancing transaction. Such suppliers are for the most part wholly unregulated as regards their insurance functions, and will remain so under EC proposals for minimum qualifications and standards for intermediaries.[42]

## Outline of UK regulatory structure

The regulation of insurance agents in the UK is a curious mix of legal and self-regulation: some rules apply to all agents, whereas others apply to agents of specific classes. The adoption of any directive along the lines of the European Commission's 1991 Recommendation on Insurance Intermediaries, discussed later in this chapter, would require a wholesale revision of domestic law.

### Rules common to all agents

UK legislation creates two criminal offences. First, any person who dishonestly or recklessly makes a false or misleading statement with the intention of inducing a contract of insurance commits a criminal offence.[43] Secondly, it is an offence for a person connected with an insurance company – by reason of shareholding, employment or agency – to fail to disclose that connection to the assured when negotiating the contract (Insurance Companies Act 1982, s 74).

### Rules applicable to insurance brokers

The governing legislation here is the Insurance Brokers (Registration) Act 1977. It is to be emphasised from the outset that this Act applies only to persons who choose to describe themselves as insurance brokers; it does not regulate the activity of insurance broking when it is carried on by persons who describe themselves in some other fashion, e.g., as insurance advisers or consultants. The Recommendation, by contrast, regulates the activity rather than the designation under which it is carried on.

---

42. See the discussion of the Commission's Recommendation on Intermediaries, below, p 90.
43. Financial Services Act 1986, ss 47 and 133.

The 1977 Act provides that any person describing himself or herself as a broker must obtain registration from the Insurance Brokers Registration Council, established under the Act. The Council is responsible for maintaining the register of brokers, for determining the qualifications and experience required for registration, and for considering individual applications. These matters are governed by Rules issued by the Council, which, taken with the Act, require a broker to have obtained either five years' experience as a broker or agent, or a recognised educational qualification coupled with three years' experience. These conditions are waived in relation to a broker who has obtained experience in an EEA member state, as the Mutual Recognition Directive, Directive 77/92, requires recognition of lesser periods of experience, and the 1977 Act simply states that any broker qualified under the Directive is entitled to be registered under the Act.[44]

A registered broker is required to adhere to the various Rules and Codes issued by the Insurance Brokers Registration Council, the most important of which relate to the conduct of investment business (1988), accounts and business requirements (1979), a general Code of Conduct (1994) and the maintenance of indemnity insurance and provision of contributions to a client compensation fund (1987). Serious lapses can lead to disciplinary proceedings and ultimately removal from the register, and thus the loss of the right to use the designation 'broker'.

Lloyd's brokers are registered under the Insurance Brokers (Registration) Act 1977 and thus are obliged to comply with its terms. Lloyd's brokers are, however, also subject to a complex set of rules contained in the Lloyd's Act 1982 and byelaws made by the Council of Lloyd's under that Act. The Lloyd's legislation is less concerned with competence than with the independence of brokers from the managing agents of the syndicates with which they place business.[45]

### Rules applicable to life intermediaries

The Financial Services Act 1986 establishes a complex regulatory structure applicable to the marketing of 'investment business', the

---

44. 1977 Act, s 3(1), (2). See p 86 below, for the detail of the Directive.
45. Lloyd's Act 1982, ss 10–12.

definition of which catches most forms of life assurance.[46] Persons wishing to carry on investment business must be authorised to do so, either directly by the Secretary of State or indirectly by seeking membership of a self-regulating organisation recognised under the Act, and thereafter are regulated by Core Business Rules laid down by the Securities and Investments Board (SIB). Those rules, in so far as they are relevant to insurance: confer upon the assured the right to cancel the policy;[47] prohibit 'cold-calling' by an agent without the assured's consent;[48] and require an agent to disclose both the nature of the contract and the amount of commission which the agent is receiving from the insurer.[49] In addition to the Core Rules, a further tier of rules has to be complied with: these may be either SIB's own rules or the rules of a self-regulating organisation. In the case of insurance, the relevant self-regulating organisation is the Personal Investment Authority (PIA).

The scheme of the Act, as applied to intermediaries, is as follows. The Act provides for 'polarisation', which means that an intermediary must be either wholly independent of all insurers, or tied exclusively to a single insurer. An independent intermediary must be authorised on his or her own behalf. A tied intermediary – referred to by the Act as an 'appointed representative' – need not be authorised, but the insurer is vicariously liable for that intermediary's acts and omissions.[50] Equally, employees of an insurance company do not require authorisation, but at common law the insurer is vicariously liable for employees in the usual way. The Rules laid down by SIB and PIA are complex and lengthy, and it suffices for present purposes to say that almost every aspect of the marketing of life policies is subject to detailed rules requiring full explanation, disclosure and fact-finding. All insurers have put into place training programmes which demand exacting standards of their appointed representatives and employees. Accordingly, it can be said that intermediaries in the life industry are heavily regulated in terms of competence and disclosure obligations.[51]

46. Financial Services Act 1986, Sched 1, para 10.
47. Financial Services (Cancellation) Rules 1989.
48. Common Unsolicited Calls Regulations 1992.
49. Financial Services (Conduct of Business) (Product and Commission Disclosure) Rules 1994.
50. Financial Services Act 1986, s 44.
51. Which does not of course mean that the structure has been an unqualified success, as the various scandals concerning the misselling of pensions and personal equity plans amply demonstrate.

*Rules applicable to other intermediaries*

There are no legal rules in place affecting the conduct or qualifications of agents falling outside the specific areas mentioned above, i.e., non-investment business conducted by persons carrying on broking business under some designation other than that of 'broker', tied agents, and employees of insurers. The gap has been filled by two Codes of Conduct, issued by the Association of British Insurers. The Code of Life Insurance (Non-Investment Business) Selling Practice for Non-Registered Intermediaries, issued in 1986, draws a distinction between 'introducers', who merely pass on applications, and other intermediaries, who are responsible for active selling. In the case of intermediaries, cold-calling must be avoided and full disclosure of policy provisions must be made to the prospective assured; in the case of introducers, whose role is more limited, advice must be accurate and limited to matters in which the introducer has competence. A second code, the General Insurance Business Code of Practice for all Intermediaries other than Registered Brokers, issued in 1989, does not draw the distinction between intermediaries and introducers, and requires all intermediaries to avoid cold-calling, to make full disclosure to the assured, and to carry liability insurance.

# The EC context: establishment, services and intermediaries

## The Mutual Recognition Directive

### Operation of the Directive

Freedom of establishment and services in respect of insurance intermediaries has been partially achieved in the EC, by means of mutual recognition of national qualifications. Council Directive 77/92, on *Measures to Facilitate the Effective Exercise of Freedom of Establishment and Freedom to Provide Services in Respect of the Activities of Insurance Brokers and Agents*, applies to three classes of intermediary: the UK designations are insurance brokers, employed and self-employed insurance agents, and sub-agents.[52] It

---

[52] Directive 77/92, art 2.

provides that where a member state requires, as a condition of taking up the activity of insurance broker or insurance agent, any general, commercial or professional knowledge and ability, that state shall accept any of the following forms of professional experience obtained in another member state as satisfying national requirements:[53]

(a) four consecutive years in an independent or managerial capacity – a managerial capacity for this purpose being the manager of an undertaking or branch, the deputy manager of an undertaking or authorised agent where the post involved responsibility equivalent to that of a manager, or the holding of duties in an insurance undertaking involving the management or supervision of agents;[54]

(b) two consecutive years in an independent or managerial capacity where the intermediary can show at least three years' experience working with an insurer or an intermediary, the relevant work having entailed responsibility in respect of the acquisition, administration and performance of contracts of insurance;[55]

(c) one year in an independent or managerial capacity where the intermediary can show that he or she has received previous training and is regarded by national or the relevant professional authorities as having satisfied its requirements.

The periods of experience obtained by the intermediary in a member state must not have ceased more than ten years before the intermediary seeks the right to pursue the activity in the host state.[56]

An intermediary who has obtained the relevant experience in another member state is entitled to apply to the authorities of the host state, and is thereafter entitled to pursue the activity of intermediary either by becoming established in the host state or by providing cross-border services in that state from an establishment in another member state. The intermediary's home authorities are required to issue a certificate to the host state confirming that the necessary qualifications have been obtained.[57] Where a host state

---

[53]. Art 4. Art 5 recognises that it is usual to impose greater controls on brokers than on employed agents, and provides that in such a case the requirements are to apply to brokers alone. The requirements are in any event shaded, by art 6, in respect of sub-agents.

[54]. The definition in art 8(1), (2).     [55]. The definition in art 8(3).     [56]. Art 7.

[57]. Art 9.

additionally requires of its own nationals proof of good repute or that the intermediary has not been declared bankrupt, such requirements may also be imposed upon an intermediary from another member state, but the host state is required to accept as proof of compliance either a document to that effect issued by the home state or, in the absence of such a document, a declaration on oath by the intermediary.[58]

The limits of the Mutual Recognition Directive are readily apparent. It does not require member states to impose minimum qualifications upon intermediaries, and it is still the case that in many member states – and to some extent this includes the UK – there is little in the way of regulation of standards and competence. Instead, the Directive merely provides that, where such qualifications are imposed by a member state, those qualifications do not operate to exclude intermediaries appropriately qualified in other member states. The Directive can, therefore, be regarded as a transitional measure, to be superseded by the eventual adoption of EC-wide qualifications and standards for intermediaries. The Directive, taken with the general anti-discrimination rules of the Treaty of Rome, in practice means no more than that: (a) where a member state does not impose any pre-entry qualifying conditions upon its own nationals who wish to be intermediaries, no conditions may be imposed upon intermediaries from other member states; and (b) where a member state does impose qualifying conditions on its own nationals, the conditions imposed upon intermediaries from other member states cannot be any more stringent and in any event they cannot exceed the minimum experience conditions laid down in the Directive. It is perfectly possible, therefore, that a member state's qualifications for its own nationals can be more onerous than those permitted by the Directive.

### UK reception

The UK did not need to legislate in order to implement the Mutual Recognition Directive, given that domestic law in its form when the Directive was adopted was in compliance. Prior to 1977 there were no conditions or qualifications to be met by any

---

58. Art 10.

intermediaries, and this continues to be the case in respect of non-life intermediaries who are not registered as brokers. The Insurance Brokers (Registration) Act 1977, described above, changed the position as regards intermediaries wishing to describe themselves as 'brokers', by imposing a registration requirement and authorising the laying down of conditions by the Insurance Brokers Registration Council as to experience and qualifications. However, the Act specifically provides that a broker who has pursued that profession for any of the periods mentioned in the Mutual Recognition Directive is entitled to be registered under the Act:[59] this is an important provision, given that the Act's provisions are more stringent than those laid down in the Directive and, as noted earlier in this chapter, require experience for five years without any qualification and three years with a qualification.[60]

Similar provisions are made for life intermediaries regulated by the Financial Services Act 1986 in respect of investment business. Only independent intermediaries are subject to direct regulation. Brokers registered under the 1977 Act automatically satisfy the authorisation requirements of the 1986 Act, and any person wishing to carry on investment business in the UK as an independent intermediary other than under the description of broker is entitled to do so on proof of equivalent authorisation in their home state.[61]

It remains the case that, outside the life industry, independent intermediaries who are not brokers, and other agents, do not require any form of national authorisation to become established or to provide cross-border services into the UK. The practical difficulty which intermediaries from other member states may face is in obtaining recognition from UK insurers, as intermediaries have to comply with the Codes of Conduct of 1986 and 1989 to achieve such recognition. However, those Codes do not lay down any rules as to qualifications or experience, and are concerned primarily with marketing practices and compulsory insurance, so that the exclusion of an EC intermediary by an insurer is unlikely to give rise to any liability on the UK for permitting an authorisation scheme to operate in contravention of the Mutual Recognition Directive.

---

59. Insurance Brokers (Registration) Act 1977, s 3(1)(c), amended by the Insurance Brokers (Registration) Act 1977 (Amendment) Order 1995, SI 1995 No 2906, art 2(2) to extend the exemption to all EEA states and not just EC states.
60. 1977 Act, s 3(1).   61. Financial Services Act 1986, s 31.

## Proposed harmonisation: the Intermediaries Recommendation

### Scope

The provisional nature of the Mutual Recognition Directive was confirmed by the European Commission's publication, in December 1991, of a recommendation on *Professional Requirements and Registration of Insurance Intermediaries*.[62] The Recommendation is, necessarily, not binding on member states, but seeks co-operation in achieving minimum standards. It is clear that the Recommendation is intended to pave the way for a full harmonisation Directive, but as of September 1996 the Commission had not commenced work on a draft.

The Recommendation has the same scope as the Mutual Recognition Directive, in that it applies to brokers, agents and sub-brokers.[63] It excludes in particular 'persons providing insurance which does not require any general or specific knowledge and where such insurance covers the risk of loss or damage to goods supplied by that person, whose principal professional activity is other than providing advice on and selling insurance'.[64] This is intended to exempt, e.g., garages providing insurance cover with their vehicles, and cif sellers, and broadly corresponds to the general category of 'other agents' identified earlier in this chapter; surprisingly, the exemption does not extend to service suppliers, such as travel agents and building societies.

The Recommendation does not seek to lay down the content of professional qualifications, and leaves the matter to member states, but sets out guiding principles against which the competence and qualifications of brokers are to be assessed. Any ensuing Directive will inevitably provide that an intermediary qualified to practise by the rules of their home state will be able to use that qualification as a 'passport' for becoming established or cross-border selling in other member states.

---

[62.] 92/48/EC. The Department of Trade and Industry published a Consultative Document in 1992 requesting views on the desirability of any change to the law. The absence of any change must presumably mean that the consultation did not produce any great demand or enthusiasm for change.
[63.] Arts 1, 2(1).   [64.] Art 2(2).

*Independence of brokers*

The Recommendation impliedly requires brokers to be independent, and to act exclusively for assureds. As seen above, the present state of English law is in broad terms consistent with that approach, although it will also be apparent that the Recommendation may need further thought if it is to deal sensibly with accepted market practices such as the operation of binding authorities by brokers.

The Recommendation expressly provides that an independent broker is to make two forms of disclosure.[65] As far as the assured or reinsured is concerned, the broker is to disclose any direct legal or economic ties to an insurance undertaking which could affect the broker's complete freedom of choice of insurance undertaking. This is to some extent the position under UK law. A life broker is, under the polarisation principle enshrined in the Financial Services Act 1986, required to be either wholly independent or wholly tied, and the Securities and Investment Board's Financial Services (Conduct of Business) (Product and Commission Disclosure) Rules 1994 require brokers to disclose the level of commission which is being received from the insurer, and the same obligations are imposed by the rules of the Personal Investment Authority. All registered brokers, life or otherwise must, under the Insurance Brokers Registration Council's Code of Conduct 1994, refrain from putting themselves into a position where duty and interest conflict, and must, on request, disclose to the assured (other than a corporate assured) the level of commission being paid by the insurer in respect of the contract.[66] More generally, regulations made under the Insurance Companies Act 1982, s 74,[67] require an intermediary, including a broker, to disclose any connection with an insurer: connection for this purpose refers to employment, shareholding or exclusive agency arrangement. It is uncertain whether the common law requires the disclosure of commission rates in situations not governed by the Insurance Brokers Registration Act 1977 and the Financial Services Act 1986 (i.e., unregistered non-life brokers): there are dicta that the corollary of the common law rule that a broker's commission is paid by the insurer is that the broker must disclose on request the amount

---

[65.] Art 3.
[66.] Principle B, and illustrations 4 and 7.
[67.] See p. 83, above.

which has been paid, although it may be that this is limited to the case in which the amount paid is excessive in relation to market norms.[68] The Recommendation is far from clear as to whether disclosure of commission rates by brokers is intended.

The second form of disclosure required is to a competent body, as designated by each member state, of the spread of business with different insurance undertakings over the previous year. What is contemplated here is some administrative supervision of the actual placing of business. There is no equivalent reporting restriction in UK law at the present, and the Insurance Brokers Registration Council does not require the provision of such information. The Recommendation does not indicate what possible sanction might apply where a broker is in practice placing business with a limited number of insurers: it remains to be seen whether any future Directive will permit investigation of the reasons for concentration and provide a mechanism for requiring spread of placement where the broker's decisions are not being made on a purely objective basis.

### Competence and professional standards

The Recommendation proposes that all insurance intermediaries are to be subject to minimum professional standards.[69] Those standards are:

(1) Possession of general, commercial and professional knowledge and ability.[70] The management of insurance intermediaries must consist of an adequate number of persons with the requisite knowledge and ability. This may be secured by direct regulation or by membership of a professional organisation. The level of knowledge and ability required is a matter for each member state. It has already been stated that in the UK it is only registered brokers and life intermediaries who are at present subject to any competence assessment, so that a change in the law would be required.

(2) Possession of adequate professional liability insurance.[71] This exists in the UK by a combination of legal provision and self-regulation: registered brokers must possess adequate liability insurance under the Insurance Brokers Registration Council's Indemnity Insurance and Grants Scheme Rules

[68.] See n 29, above.   [69.] Art 4(1).   [70.] Arts 2(4) and 4(2).   [71.] Art 4(3).

1987; life brokers must be insured under the rules of the Securities and Investments Board, while insurance companies are vicariously liable for the misdeeds of appointed agents and employees,[72] and the Compensation of Investors Rules 1994 made by the Securities and Investments Board in any event provide a fall back guarantee for investors; and other intermediaries are required to carry liability insurance by the Association of British Insurers' Codes of Conduct 1986 (life) and 1989 (non-life).

(3) Good repute, and not in undischarged bankruptcy. Existing UK law guarantees these matters as regards registered brokers[73] and life intermediaries,[74] although there is no restriction in respect of unregistered brokers and other intermediaries other than the unwillingness of insurers to deal with such persons.

(4) In the case of brokers, possession of sufficient financial capacity, to be determined by member states.[75] In the UK, this requirement at present applies only to registered brokers.[76]

*Registration*

The Recommendation provides that registration is a precondition of a person being allowed to pursue the activity of insurance intermediary, and that registration is to be confined to persons meeting the competence and professional standards requirements to be ascertained by member states.[77] This proposal would require a major change to UK law. As things stand in the UK, registration is open only to brokers and not to other intermediaries, and even then the Insurance Brokers Registration Act 1977 does not demand registration but merely provides that registration – which

---

72. Financial Services Act 1986, s 44.
73. Insurance Brokers Registration Act 1977, s 3(2) – good character and suitability a precondition of registration.
74. By means of the authorisation procedure whereby authorisation must be sought directly from the Secretary of State or by membership of a self-regulating organisation – in either case, fitness for the role is a precondition. Appointed representatives and employees are not subject to any such requirement as a matter of law, but, given that insurers are vicariously liable for their misconduct, this exists as a matter of practice.
75. Art 4(4).
76. Under the Insurance Brokers Registration Council's Accounts and Business Requirements Rules 1979.
77. Art 5.

of itself attracts regulation by the Insurance Brokers Registration Council – is an essential qualification for the use of the description 'broker'.[78] The Recommendation, if implemented, would replace the UK's curious system of having close regulation of persons calling themselves 'brokers' but, outside the life industry and disregarding Codes of Conduct laid down by insurers themselves, no formal regulation of unregistered intermediaries.

[78.] Insurance Brokers Registration Act 1977, s 22.

# CHAPTER FIVE

# Jurisdiction in insurance and reinsurance disputes

## Introduction

### Significance of jurisdiction

This chapter explains the EC rules for determining which court (or 'forum') has jurisdiction to hear an insurance or reinsurance dispute. The question of which forum has jurisdiction is important for litigants for various reasons. First, there are practical differences between fora, such as the speed and expense of bringing proceedings there, the experience and perhaps sympathies of the judiciary, and the convenience to the parties. Secondly, the forum's procedural rules may determine issues such as which party bears the burden of proof, whether the parties are obliged to provide documentary discovery, and what types of remedy are available. Thirdly, courts have varying approaches to determining which substantive law applies: if, for example, the parties to a contract agree that the contract is to be governed by French law, their choice might be upheld by some courts but disregarded by others (EC courts' rules for determining the applicable law have largely been harmonised as will be seen in chapter 6). Fourthly, the place where the judgment is given will affect the enforceability of the judgment against the defendant's assets.

### The Brussels Convention

By art 220(4) of the EEC Treaty the member states undertook to enter into negotiations with each other to simplify the formalities for the recognition and enforcement of judgments. Until then, these matters had been dealt with by an *ad hoc* network of

bilateral conventions between member states together with various multilateral conventions relating to specialised matters.

The first steps towards harmonisation were taken in 1960 when the then six member states started negotiations to produce a convention whereby a judgment handed down in the courts of one member state would be enforceable as of right in any of the other member states. As the member states would be curtailing their right to review the validity of judgments which could be enforced in their territories, it was also considered necessary to ensure that each of the member states would assume jurisdiction only on a proper and justified basis. To this end, a uniform set of rules was devised for any member state to determine whether it had jurisdiction. The rules for the allocation of jurisdiction have had a far greater impact than the rule requiring recognition of judgments and it may fairly be said that 'the tail has wagged the dog'.[1]

The result of the negotiations was the Convention on Jurisdiction and the Enforcement of Judgments in Civil and Commercial Matters[2] (hereafter 'the Brussels Convention' or 'the Convention') which was signed by the original six member states in 1968. Other member states subsequently acceded to the Convention, and its provisions were amended by each of the accession conventions.[3] Which jurisdiction rules apply in a particular case will depend on which version of the rules was in force in the relevant member state at the time the proceedings were instituted. The dates of ratification and entry into force of the original Convention and the various accession conventions are set out in Appendix 1. In English law the Brussels Convention (as amended) is implemented by the Civil Jurisdiction and Judgments Act 1982 (as amended).

The Convention was concluded for an unlimited period.[4] Any

---

1. K.M. Newman, 'Background and Scheme of the Civil Jurisdiction and Judgments Act 1982' in *Jurisdiction and Enforcement of Judgments in Europe* (College of Law, 1985), p. 4.
2. OJ 1978 L304/36.
3. The Luxembourg Convention on the accession of the United Kingdom, Denmark and Ireland (OJ 1978 L304/1); the Greek accession convention (OJ 1982 L388/1); and the San Sebastián Convention on the accession of Portugal and Spain (OJ 1989 L285/1). The text of the latest amended version of the Convention is at OJ 1990 C189/1 (but see p 119 below). Where the Convention's provisions have been amended by the accession conventions this is identified in the text although many of the changes are of little relevance to insurance and reinsurance cases. The convention for the accession of Austria, Finland and Sweden (see p 97) has not yet been ratified.
4. Article 66.

member state may request the revision of its rules, in which circumstance a revision conference would be convened.[5]

## The Lugano Convention

In 1988 a convention was opened for signature by the representatives of the then twelve EC member states[6] and six EFTA states.[7] This convention was largely identical to the Brussels Convention (as amended) and it is thus often referred to as the 'parallel convention'. The dates of ratification and entry into force of the Lugano Convention are set out in Appendix 2. Its provisions are implemented in English law by the Civil Jurisdiction and Judgments Act 1991.[8]

In states which have implemented both the Brussels and Lugano conventions, the Lugano Convention applies where (i) the defendant is domiciled in a contracting state which is not a member of the EC, (ii) a jurisdiction clause selects the courts of such a state, or (iii) the court has to decide whether to decline jurisdiction on the basis that proceedings have already been started in such a state.[9]

Since joining the Community Austria, Finland and Sweden have implemented the Lugano Convention but not the Brussels Convention (the most significant consequence of which is that these states' courts cannot refer questions of interpretation to the European Court of Justice – see 'Interpretation' below). A convention for the accession of these states to the Brussels Convention was signed by all 15 member states on 29 November 1996 (although at the time of writing it has not been ratified).

## Scope of the Brussels Convention

There are a number of limitations on the scope of the Convention.

First, it applies only to civil and commercial matters.[10] The European Court of Justice has held that claims concerning the acts of public bodies in the exercise of their public law powers are not

---

5. Article 67.
6. Belgium, Denmark, France, Germany, Greece, Ireland, Italy, Luxembourg, the Netherlands, Portugal, Spain and the United Kingdom.
7. Austria, Finland, Iceland, Norway, Sweden and Switzerland.
8. Amending the Civil Jurisdiction and Judgments Act 1982.
9. Lugano Convention, Article 54B.
10. Article 1.

'civil' matters[11] and claims brought by or against public bodies may therefore fall outside the Convention.

Secondly, it applies only where the dispute contains an international element.[12] The international element would probably be lacking where, for example, an insurer and insured, both domiciled in France, concluded a contract insuring goods situated in France, and one of the parties sued the other in the French courts. If, however, the contract contained a choice of English jurisdiction,[13] or if the parties were domiciled in different contracting states, the Convention would apply. To determine jurisdiction as between the different parts of the United Kingdom, the UK government has implemented an additional set of rules closely modelled on the Convention.[14]

Thirdly, many of its rules apply only if the defendant is domiciled in a contracting state. If the defendant is not domiciled in a contracting state then the court must apply its own rules to determine whether it has jurisdiction.[15] However, some of the Convention's rules apply regardless of the defendant's domicile.[16] In some circumstances insurers may be deemed to be domiciled in a contracting state by virtue of having a branch, agency or other establishment there.[17]

Fourthly, it does not affect specialised conventions which contain jurisdiction rules,[18] for example the convention on the contract for the international carriage of goods by road ('CMR').

Finally, it does not apply to insolvency proceedings[19] or 'arbitration'.[20] The arbitration exclusion is particularly important in the context of reinsurance, as such contracts frequently include arbitration clauses. It is clear that the Convention does not determine the place where an arbitration should be heard or the

---

11. Case 29/76 *LTU Lufttransportunternehmen GmbH & Co KG v Eurocontrol* [1976] ECR 1541 at p 1551; Case 814/79 *Netherlands State v Reinhold Rüffer* [1980] ECR 3807 at p 3819.

12. Preamble to the Convention; report by Jenard, OJ 1979 C59/1 at p 8.

13. Report by Jenard, OJ 1979 C59/1 at p 38.

14. Civil Jurisdiction and Judgments Act 1982, Sched 4.

15. Article 4. These rules must not discriminate on the basis of the plaintiff's nationality.

16. The most notable such provisions appear to be arts 17 (jurisdiction agreements), 18 (submission to jurisdiction) and arts 21 and 22 (priority of identical or related actions brought in different contracting states), but see pp 126–7.

17. Article 8, second paragraph (as amended by the Luxembourg Convention). See p 114.

18. Article 57.   19. Article 1(2).   20. Article 1(4).

courts which have jurisdiction in matters such as the appointment[21] or removal of arbitrators. But there are two issues which are less than clear. The first is whether the Convention determines which courts have jurisdiction to consider the validity of an arbitration clause. The second is whether the fact that a contract contains an arbitration clause removes any dispute on the substance of the contract from the ambit of the Convention.

In *The Atlantic Emperor*[22] a seller brought proceedings in Italy against a buyer on a contract of sale. The buyer applied to the English court for an order appointing an arbitrator pursuant to a purported arbitration clause in the contract. The seller argued before the English court that the Convention applied to the English proceedings (with the consequence that the English court would probably have been obliged to decline jurisdiction pursuant to art 21).[23] The Court of Appeal referred this question to the European Court of Justice, which held[24] that the applicability of the arbitration exclusion depended on the subject matter of the dispute. Where the subject matter, such as the appointment of an arbitrator, was excluded then the Convention did not apply, regardless of whether the court was also required to consider other preliminary issues such as the validity of the arbitration agreement. Thus the Convention did not apply to determine whether or not the English court had jurisdiction.

Because the Court of Justice's decision was drawn in very narrow terms it did little to resolve the general uncertainty about the extent of the arbitration exclusion. In the English case *The Heidberg*[25] Judge Diamond QC was called upon to consider whether a judgment of a French court, which had held that the wording of a bill of lading had not been effective to incorporate an arbitration agreement, was within the Convention (the consequence being that if the judgment was within the Convention it would have to be recognised by the English court). The judge considered that it was 'beyond doubt' that a judgment of a foreign court on the substance of a dispute, even if given in breach of a valid arbitration agreement, was within the scope of the

---

21. Case C-190/89 *Marc Rich & Co AG v Società Italiana Impianti PA (The Atlantic Emperor)* [1991] ECR I-3855 (ECJ) at p 3901.
22. *Marc Rich & Co AG v Società Italiana Impianti PA*; see note 21 above.
23. See pp 123–5.    24. At pp 3901–4.
25. *Partenreederei M/S Heidberg v Grosvenor Grain and Feed Co Ltd* [1994] 2 Lloyd's Rep 287.

Convention. As regards foreign rulings on the validity or otherwise of an arbitration clause, he took the view, principally for 'practical and policy reasons',[26] that such judgments were also within the Convention. This approach was, in his view, less likely to lead to conflicting judgments than the alternative one. However, as Judge Diamond recognised,[27] conflicts might still occur: for example, the situation may arise where the Italian courts have jurisdiction to hear the substantive dispute whilst the English courts have jurisdiction to hear proceedings for the appointment of an arbitrator. In a later case[28] Rix J explained the decision in The Heidberg on the basis that the dispute's essential subject matter was the construction of the contract rather than a 'pure question of arbitration'.[29]

The same questions were addressed again in the recent case Philip Alexander Securities and Futures Limited v Bamberger and others.[30] Investors brought proceedings in Germany against a futures and options broker in respect of trading losses. The contracts between the investors and the broker contained London arbitration clauses. The German courts ruled that the arbitration clauses were invalid as a matter of construction or under German consumer protection laws and found in the investors' favour on the merits of their claims. In the subsequent proceedings in England Waller J considered the extent to which the English court was bound to recognise the German judgments. He agreed with the view expressed by Judge Diamond in The Heidberg that a judgment on the substance of a dispute was a Convention judgment. Regarding the question whether the ruling on the validity of the arbitration agreement was within the Convention, Waller J was strongly inclined to take the view that where (at least in part) one was dealing with the invalidity of an arbitration clause as found by the local law the decision was outside the Convention, whether ruled on at a preliminary stage or together with a judgment on the substance of the dispute. This approach would, he said, allow the English courts to take a flexible approach whereby they could grant an injunction against a party who started proceedings abroad in contravention of the arbitration agreement, and then refuse to

---

26. At p 303.    27. At pp 301–2.
28. Qingdao Ocean Shipping Co v Grace Shipping Establishment Transatlantic Schiffahrtskontor GmbH, The Xing Su Hai [1995] 2 Lloyd's Rep 15.
29. At p 21.    30. 2 May 1996, unreported.

recognise any subsequent judgment on the substance of the dispute on the grounds that it was contrary to the public policy of the United Kingdom[31] or that the judgment was irreconcilable with a previous judgment of the English court.[32] Thus a judgment on the merits, whilst being within the Convention, might well not be recognisable if obtained in breach of an arbitration provision. On appeal,[33] the Court of Appeal agreed with the German courts as to the invalidity of the arbitration agreements and it was therefore unnecessary for it to determine whether or not the German decisions in this regard were within the Convention: Leggatt LJ stated that if it had been necessary to answer this question it would have been appropriate to refer it to the European Court of Justice. The Court of Appeal did not overturn Waller J's decision regarding the German decisions on the merits. As Judge Diamond observed in *The Heidberg*,[34] the extent of the exclusion is a 'vexed question' and it seems inevitable that it will be referred to the Court of Justice in due course.[34a]

## Interpretation

In order to ensure that the Convention's rules are applied consistently throughout the Community contracting states may (and often do) refer questions of interpretation to the Court of Justice.[35] The Convention must be interpreted in accordance with the Court's decisions.[36] (The Lugano Convention does not contain any procedure for questions to be referred to the Court of Justice, but its provisions are likely to be interpreted consistently with those of the Brussels Convention.[37]) The official reports on the

31. Pursuant to Art 27(1) of the Convention.
32. Pursuant to Art 27(3).
33. 12 July 1996, unreported.
34. [1994] 2 Lloyd's Rep 287 at pp 297–8.
34a. The authorities have been reviewed by Clarke J in *Union de Remorquage v Lake Avery, The Lake Avery*, 4 November 1996 (unreported). The judge said that 'the correct test is whether the relief sought ... can fairly be said to be ancillary to, or perhaps an integral part of the arbitration process', but recognised that 'there will often be a narrow line between a case which falls within the exception and a case which does not'.
35. Protocol to the Convention the original version of which was signed in 1971. The latest version of the Protocol (as amended by the accession conventions) is at OJ 1990 C189/25.
36. Civil Jurisdiction and Judgments Act 1982, s 3(1), (2).
37. The official report on the Lugano Convention by Jenard and Möller (OJ 1990 C189/57) states (at p 89) that the Lugano Convention should be interpreted

Brussels Convention[38] and the accession conventions[39] may also be used as aids to interpretation[40] although they are not binding.

The Convention has been drawn up in ten[41] different language versions. Where these versions differ, each version must be accorded equal weight.[42] The Convention must be interpreted to give effect to its intentions (the 'purposive' or 'teleological' method) rather than in a strictly literal way.

## Outline of the Convention's jurisdictional rules

The Convention contains one set of jurisdictional rules which is of general application and another which applies to insurance matters. It is probable (but not certain) that reinsurance falls within the general rules (see below). These rules are considered in detail below, but it may be helpful to give an outline at this stage.

Under the general rules (arts 2 to 6a[43]) the plaintiff may sue the defendant in the contracting state in which the defendant is domiciled. Alternatively the plaintiff may bring proceedings in the contracting state where the contractual obligation was to be performed, where the tort occurred, or (in cases arising out of the operations of a branch or agency) where the branch or agency is situated.

The special insurance rules (arts 7 to 11) are designed to protect policyholders. Under these rules an insurer may be sued in the contracting state in which (i) it is domiciled, (ii) the policyholder is domiciled or (iii) the leading insurer is sued (if it is a co-insurer). Actions by the insurer against the insured must usually be brought in the contracting state where the insured is domiciled. Additional provisions deal with multiparty actions and liability and property insurance.

---

37. *(continued)* consistently with the judgments of the Court of Justice, and a Protocol (OJ 1988 L319/31) requires the contracting states to take due account of the decisions of each other's courts. See also the Joint Declarations at OJ 1988 L319/37 and 40.

38. Jenard, OJ 1979 C59/1.

39. Schlosser, OJ 1979 C59/71 (Luxembourg Convention); Evrigenis and Kerameus, OJ 1986 C298/1 (Greek accession convention); de Almeida Cruz, Desantes Real and Jenard, OJ 1990 C189/35 (San Sebastián Convention).

40. Civil Jurisdiction and Judgments Act 1982, s 3(3).

41. Twelve including Finnish and Swedish.

42. Article 68, as amended by the Luxembourg Convention, the Greek accession convention and the San Sebastián Convention.

43. Article 6a was inserted by the Luxembourg Convention.

The parties may overrule the above rules by agreeing which forum is to hear their disputes (art 17[44]) although in relation to insurance matters their ability to do so is circumscribed (arts 12[45] and 12a[46]).

The Convention's rules sometimes give jurisdiction to the courts of more than one contracting state. In such circumstances the Convention provides a procedure (arts 21[47] to 23) to prevent the same or related claims from being heard in more than one forum.

## Do the special insurance rules apply to reinsurance matters?

The Convention does not make it clear whether the insurance rules apply only to direct insurance or whether they also cover reinsurance. The relevant part of the Convention, Title II Section 3, is headed simply 'Jurisdiction in matters relating to insurance'.

As a matter of principle it would seem appropriate that these rules should apply only to direct insurance, since the policyholder protection which they provide is inappropriate to reinsurance transactions. This view is supported by the official report on the Luxembourg Convention which states, 'Reinsurance contracts cannot be equated with insurance contracts. Accordingly, arts 7 to 12 do not apply to reinsurance contracts.'[48] There is also English judicial authority to this effect. In *Trade Indemnity plc and others v Försäkringsaktiebolaget Njord (in liquidation)*[49] Rix J, considering the identical insurance provisions in the Lugano Convention, expressed the view[50] that the provisions do not apply to reinsurance, and stated that the European Court of Justice would be 'highly likely' to reach this conclusion in relation to the Brussels Convention.[51]

---

44. As amended by the Luxembourg Convention and the San Sebastián Convention.
45. As amended by the Luxembourg Convention.
46. Inserted by the Luxembourg Convention.
47. As amended by the San Sebastián Convention.
48. OJ 1979 C59/71 at p 117, para 151.
49. [1995] 1 All ER 796.
50. At p 804.
51. See also *Citadel Insurance Co v Atlantic Union Insurance Co SA* [1982] 2 Lloyd's Rep 543 at p 549 (CA) *per* Kerr LJ and *Arkwright Mutual Insurance Co v Bryanston Insurance Co Ltd* [1990] 2 QB 649, [1990] 2 Lloyd's Rep 70 at p 73 *per* Potter J.

However in *New Hampshire Insurance Co v Strabag Bau AG*[52] Lloyd LJ stated that he did 'not think it would be right' to assume that reinsurance is outside the scope of the insurance section until the Court of Justice has so ruled. Unfortunately, on the only occasion when the question has been referred to the Court of Justice[53] the case was disposed of on other grounds without any findings being made on the point. In its written observations submitted to the Court on that occasion the Commission remarked[54] that

> It is difficult to see any fundamental difference between insurance and reinsurance which could justify exclusion of reinsurance contracts from the scope of Section 3 of Title II. As a more general matter, since the Convention is designed precisely to avoid and resolve conflicts of jurisdiction, any exclusion of such a substantial nature would need to be expressly stated in the text of the Convention, and not merely inferred.

It seems likely that the Court of Justice would find that reinsurance is governed by the general provisions and the rest of this chapter assumes this to be the case. It is, however, unfortunate that there is no more decisive authority on this important point.

# Rules which apply in the absence of a valid jurisdiction agreement

## The general rules (reinsurance)

The Convention's general jurisdictional rules are contained in Title II Sections 1 and 2 (arts 2 to 6a[55]). The starting point is that the defendant must usually be sued in the contracting state in which he or she is domiciled, regardless of nationality (art 2). Thus if a French-domiciled reinsured brings proceedings in England against its English-domiciled reinsurer the English court would have jurisdiction. A corporation or association[56] is domiciled where it

---

52. [1992] 1 Lloyd's Rep 361 at p 369.
53. Case C-351/89 *Overseas Union Insurance Limited v New Hampshire Insurance Company* [1991] ECR I-3317.
54. [1991] ECR I-3333.
55. Article 6a was inserted by the Luxembourg Convention.
56. There is some doubt about whether the domicile of a partnership is to be determined by these rules or the rules relating to the domicile of an individual (as to which see p 98 and p 112. In Scotland a Lloyd's syndicate has been assumed to be an association for these purposes: *Davenport v Corinthian Motor Policies at Lloyd's* 1991 SLT 774 at pp 776 and 779.

has its seat. The court must identify this location by applying its own law.[57] Under English law[58] a corporation is domiciled in a particular state for these purposes if (i) it was incorporated or formed under that state's law and it has its registered office or some other official address there, or (ii) its central management and control is exercised there.[59]

In certain circumstances the plaintiff may choose to sue in a different forum. These circumstances are considered below.

### Matters relating to a contract

In 'matters relating to a contract', the plaintiff may sue in the courts for 'the place of performance of the obligation in question' (art 5(1)).[60] The Court of Justice has held[61] that 'the obligation in question' means (except in employment cases) the obligation which forms the basis of the plaintiff's claim. Thus where the dispute relates to non-payment of a claim, the obligation in question is the obligation to make payment.

> Example: A German reinsurer refuses to pay a claim made by an English reinsured. The contract is governed by English law. Under English law payment is usually presumed to be due at the payee's address.[62] Article 5(1) would therefore permit the reinsured to sue for payment in the English courts.

In connection with this example, it should be noted that this presumption of English law is rebuttable. If, for example, the court were persuaded that the reinsurer was required to make payments at the broker's business address then the member state indicated by art 5(1) would be the state in which the broker had its place of business.[63]

---

57. Article 53.  58. Civil Jurisdiction and Judgments Act 1982, s 42.
59. However a corporation will not be regarded as having its seat in another contracting state if it is shown that the courts of that state would not regard it as having its seat there: s 42(7).
60. The French and Dutch texts of article 5(1) were amended by the Luxembourg Convention. The Article was further amended by the San Sebastián Convention. Luxembourg domiciliaries may refuse to submit to jurisdiction founded by art 5(1) (Protocol to the Convention, art I).
61. Case 14/76 *Ets. A. de Bloos, SPRL v Société en commandite par actions Bouyer* [1976] ECR 1497; Case 266/85 *Hassan Shenavai v Klaus Kreischer* [1987] ECR 239.
62. Dicey & Morris, *The Conflict of Laws*, 12th edn (Sweet & Maxwell, 1993), at p 336.
63. In *Citadel Insurance Co. v Atlantic Union Insurance Co. SA* [1982] 2 Lloyd's Rep 543 a London broker operated the cover under which the reinsurance was

There has been some doubt regarding the application of art 5(1) to claims for the avoidance of contracts and to claims for restitution of premiums paid under contracts which are subsequently avoided *ab initio*.

In *Trade Indemnity plc v Försäkringsaktiebølaget Njord (in liquidation)*[64] reinsurers in the London market brought proceedings for a declaration of avoidance for misrepresentation and non-disclosure by the reinsured. The proceedings were brought in England pursuant to art 5(1) on the ground that the relevant obligation, to make a fair presentation of the risk, was to be performed there. Rix J held that the claim for avoidance was a matter relating to a contract and he was inclined to take the view (although the question was not directly in issue) that a claim for restitution of premium would also be. However, on the basis that art 5(1) was intended to give jurisdiction to the place where the contract was to be performed rather than the place where it was made, Rix J held that the pre-contractual duty to make a fair presentation could not constitute the obligation in question.

Subsequently the Court of Appeal handed down two judgments which considered the application of art 5(1) in cases where a contract had, or allegedly had, never come into existence. Although neither of these cases concerned reinsurance the principles are of general application. In *Kleinwort Benson Ltd v Glasgow City Council* the defendant had entered into an agreement without having the legal capacity to do so. Consequently, although the parties had intended to create a contract the operation of law precluded a contract from having come into being. The plaintiff brought a claim for restitution of money paid under the void contract and the Court of Appeal was asked to

---

63. *(continued)* placed and drew up regular settlement statements. Kerr LJ held (at p 548) that there could be no question of the defendants making payment except through the broker and that the breach therefore occurred in England. In *Cantieri Navali Riuniti S.p.A. v N.V. Omne Justitia, The Stolt Marmaro* [1985] 2 Lloyd's Rep 428 (CA) at p 436 Goff LJ found that the usual presumption applied in the absence of a contractual term or evidence of a binding practice to the contrary. In *Crédit Lyonnais v New Hampshire Insurance Company*, 16 September 1996 unreported, two insurance policies provided cover to the UK branch or subsidiary of a multinational company. The policies contained an express provision that premiums were payable through the broker in England and there was a logical inference that claims would be made and paid in England. Miss B. Dohmann QC, sitting as a Deputy Judge in the Commercial Court, appeared to accept the argument that these facts established performance in England.

64. [1995] 1 All ER 796.

determine whether this claim was properly classed as a matter relating to a contract for the purposes of art 5(1). (The court initially referred this question to the Court of Justice but the Court of Justice declined to provide an answer, stating that it had no jurisdiction to answer the question since it arose in the context of an intra-UK dispute.[65]) The Court of Appeal held[66] by a majority (Leggatt LJ dissenting) that a broad interpretation should be given to art 5(1) and that a dispute concerning an agreement which was intended to be binding but which, for legal reasons, was not a valid contract could still be a 'matter relating to a contract'. In *Boss Group Ltd v Boss France SA*[67] the Court of Appeal held that art 5(1) could still apply where the plaintiff alleged that no contract existed and the defendant argued that there was a contract.

Mance J reconsidered the above authorities at length in *Ian Charles Agnew v Lansforsakringsbolagens AB*.[68] As in *Trade Indemnity v Försäkrings*, reinsurers in the London market sued in England for declarations of avoidance on the grounds that they had been induced to enter reinsurance contracts by the reinsured's misrepresentations. In the light of *Trade Indemnity* the reinsured accepted that the claim for avoidance was a matter relating to a contract and Mance J stated that this acceptance was well-founded since the claims were 'on any objective appreciation intimately concerned with and closely related to the contracts'. However, the defendants, citing the *Trade Indemnity* judgment for support, argued that for the purposes of art 5(1) the duty to make a fair presentation could not constitute the obligation in question. Mance J disagreed. He considered that once it is ascertained that the matter relates to a contract, the only enquiry required for art 5(1) to be effective is whether the matter involves an obligation: to distinguish between pre- and post-contractual duties was looking at matters 'too broadly and from the wrong angle in the context of the Convention'. Thus the duty to make a fair presentation of the risk was capable of being the 'obligation in question'. In the judge's view the place of performance of the duty to make a fair presentation offered 'a sensible and convenient' jurisdiction which would not impair the effectiveness of the Convention.

---

65. Case C-346/93, [1995] ECR I-615.  66. [1996] 2 WLR 655.
67. *The Times*, 15 April 1996.
68. 30 July 1996, unreported. *Trade Indemnity v Försäkrings* and *Agnew v Lansforsakrings* both concerned the Lugano Convention.

The balance of English authority is therefore that where the claim is for either a declaration that a contract was never concluded or has been validly avoided or for restitution of payments made pursuant to a void contract, the matter falls within art 5(1).

### Matters relating to tort

In matters relating to tort, the plaintiff may sue in the courts for 'the place where the harmful event occurred' (art 5(3)). In *Handelskwekerij G.J. Bier B.V. v Mines de Potasse d'Alsace SA*[69] the Court of Justice held that this provision entitles a plaintiff to bring proceedings in either (a) the place where the act was committed or (b) the place where the damage was suffered, at his or her option.

*(a) Place where the act was committed* Where a reinsured negligently or intentionally breaches its duty to make a fair presentation of the risk it is arguable that the reinsurer may be able to rely on art 5(3) to found jurisdiction in the place where the negligent act was committed[70] (although the recent English authorities suggest that the proper ground of jurisdiction in such circumstances is art 5(1)).

In *Minster Investments Ltd v Hyundai Precision & Industry Co Ltd*,[71] a claim in relation to payments made in reliance upon negligently-produced certificates, Steyn J held[72] that the event which caused harm to the English plaintiffs was their receipt of the statements which the defendants intended them to rely on, and that the place where the harmful event occurred was therefore England. In the context of reinsurance, a reinsurer might therefore argue that the tort occurred in the place where it received the reinsured's presentation.

*(b) Place where the damage was suffered* The *Bier* case concerned physical damage (seed beds in the Netherlands damaged by saline waste released into the Rhine in France), but in most reinsurance cases the 'damage' will be purely financial loss. Whether *Bier* gives jurisdiction to the courts of the place where

---

69. Case 21/76, [1976] ECR 1735.
70. See *Trade Indemnity plc v Försäkringsaktiebolaget Njord (in liquidation)* [1995] 1 All ER 796 at p 820.
71. [1988] 2 Lloyd's Rep 621.   72. At p 624.

financial damage is suffered has been a vexed question but a number of principles have emerged from recent cases.

It appears that financial loss is capable of constituting the damage required to found jurisdiction under this head. In *Société Commerciale de Réassurance v ERAS International Ltd (The ERAS EIL actions)*[73] an underwriting agent's acts exposed a pool manager to claims in the English courts which, if successful, would have resulted in judgments enforceable against the manager in England. The Court of Appeal held[74] that damage was suffered in England 'in a real sense' and that the English courts had jurisdiction.[75]

However if the initial damage occurs in one state the plaintiff cannot sue in another state merely because the plaintiff ultimately feels indirect financial consequences there. To hold otherwise would almost invariably entitle the plaintiff to sue in their home state, which would be contrary to the Convention's principle that defendants should generally be sued in the state of their domicile.[76]

In practice, identifying the place where non-physical damage initially occurs is likely to prove troublesome.[77]

*Disputes arising out of a branch, agency or other establishment*

As regards a dispute arising out of the operations of a branch, agency or other establishment, the plaintiff may sue in the courts for the place in which the branch, agency or other establishment is situated (art 5(5)). The Court of Justice has held[78] that a 'branch, agency or other establishment' exists only if the entity in question is under the direction and control of a parent body, has a management, and is materially equipped to negotiate business with third parties on behalf of the parent (which must be domiciled in a

---

73. [1992] 1 Lloyd's Rep 570.     74. At p 591 (Mustill LJ).
75. See also Case C-68/93 *Fiona Shevill v Presse Alliance SA* [1995] ECR I-415 at p 460, para 23.
76. Case C-220/88 *Dumez France and Tracoba v Hessische Landesbank (Helaba)* [1990] ECR I-49; Case C-364/93 *Antonio Marinari v Lloyds Bank plc (Zubaidi Trading Co, intervener)* [1995] ECR I-2719; see also Advocate General Warner's opinion in Case 814/79 *Netherlands State v Reinhold Rüffer* [1980] ECR 3807 at p 3836 (case decided on other grounds), and *The ERAS EIL actions* (n 73 above) at p 591.
77. See, for example, *Kitechnology BV v Unicor GmbH Rahn Plastmaschinen* [1994] ILPr 560 (Millett J) and 568 (CA).
78. Case 14/76 *Ets. A. de Bloos, SPRL v Société en commandite par actions Bouyer* [1976] ECR 1497, and Case 33/78 *Somafer SA v Saar-Ferngas AG* [1978] ECR 2183.

member state[79]). It must also have the appearance of permanency. An independent commercial agent does not satisfy the requirement of being under the parent's direction and control if it is free to represent several rival firms marketing similar products, if it is free to organise its own work without being subject to instructions from the parent body, or if it does not participate in the completion and execution of transactions but merely transmits the client's orders.[80]

It will therefore be seen that independent insurance brokers are not 'agencies' within the meaning of this Article.[81] This has been confirmed in the English case *New Hampshire Insurance Co v Strabag Bau AG*.[82] Thus if a German reinsured, through its London broker, failed to disclose material facts to its reinsurer, this Article would not entitle the reinsurer to rely on the broker's address to bring proceedings in England.

### Related actions

Article 6[83] entitles the plaintiff to sue the defendant in a court where related proceedings are brought. There are three relevant provisions.

*(a) Multiple defendants (art 6(1))* Where the defendant is one of a number of defendants, he or she may be sued in the courts for the place where any one of them is domiciled. So, for example, where a contract of reinsurance is led by a company domiciled in England and the following reinsurers are domiciled in Germany, the reinsured could bring proceedings against all the reinsurers in Germany or England.

It might be thought that a plaintiff could abuse this provision by joining a second defendant for the sole purpose of suing the 'true' defendant in a state where that defendant is not domiciled. However, the Court of Justice has ruled[83] that this provision may

---

79. Article 5, first paragraph.
80. Case 139/80 *Blanckaert & Willems PVBA v Luise Trost* [1981] ECR 819 at p 829.
81. The official report by Jenard states that, in relation to insurance, art 5(5) applies 'when the foreign company is represented by a person able to conclude contracts with third parties on behalf of the company' (OJ 1979 C59/1 at p 31). In the light of the Court of Justice's decisions this statement appears to be too broad. The official report on the Luxembourg Convention by Schlosser states that the provision does not apply to independent insurance brokers (OJ 1979 C59/71 at p 116, para 150).
82. [1990] 2 Lloyd's Rep 61 at pp 68–9 (Potter J).
83. Article 6 was amended by the San Sebastián Convention.
84. Case 189/89 *Athanasios Kalfelis v Bankhaus Schröder* [1988] ECR 5565 at pp 5583–4.

be used only where the claim against the additional defendant is 'related', in the sense that it would be expedient to hear the claims together to avoid the risk of irreconcilable judgments. Where the claim against one of the defendants is clearly untenable there is little or no risk of an irreconcilable judgment being given.[85]

*(b) Third party proceedings (art 6(2))*[86]  Third party proceedings may be brought in the same courts as the original claim. For example, if a reinsurer brings an action in England against the reinsured, seeking a declaration of avoidance on the grounds of the re-insured's failure to disclose a material fact, the reinsured might wish to sue its broker for having failed to pass on all the necessary information. Regardless of the domicile of the broker, the re-insured could bring the proceedings against the broker in the English courts. Again, this provision does not apply if the main proceedings were started solely to found jurisdiction against the third party.

*(c) Counterclaims (art 6(3))*  A counterclaim may be brought in the court where the original claim is pending. The counterclaim must arise from the same contract or facts on which the original claim was based. Thus if a reinsured sues its reinsurer in England in respect of an unpaid claim, the reinsurer could bring an action for a declaration of avoidance in the same court. This provision applies only to counterclaims (i.e., where the defendant seeks the pronouncement of a separate judgment or decree) and not where the defendant raises a claim which is purely a defence.[87]

## Jurisdictional rules which apply in insurance matters

Title II Section 3 (arts 7 to 12a[88]) of the Convention deals with jurisdiction in matters relating to insurance. The choice of fora available to a plaintiff is different from that under the general

---

85. *Qingdao Ocean Shipping Co v Grace Shipping Establishment Transatlantic Shiffahrtskontor GmbH, The Xing Su Hai* [1995] 2 Lloyd's Rep 15 at p 22 (*per* Rix J). In addition, English civil procedure requires that the plaintiff demonstrate that there is a seriously arguable claim against each of the defendants: *The Xing Su Hai* at p 22 and *The Rewia* [1991] 2 Lloyd's Rep 325 (CA).

86. This provision is not applicable in Germany or Austria (Protocol to the Brussels Convention, article V (as amended)).

87. Case C-341/93 *Danværn Production A/S v Schuhfabriken Otterbeck GmbH & Co* [1995] ECR I-2053.

88. Articles 12 (amended by the Luxembourg Convention) and 12a (inserted by the Luxembourg Convention), which concern the validity of jurisdiction clauses, are considered separately at pp 115–22 below.

rules. An insurer must usually sue its insured in the state where the insured is domiciled, whilst the insured may sue the insurer in the insurer's or the insured's state. This is a 'consumerist' measure to protect insureds. Where the insurer is pursuing a subrogated or assigned claim against a third party who caused the loss (and is effectively suing in the place of the insured) the claim is probably not a matter 'relating to insurance' and the general jurisdiction rules (i.e., arts 2 to 6a, discussed above) will apply.

Title II Section 3 differentiates between 'policyholder', 'insured' and 'beneficiary'. No definitions are provided, but the official reports[89] indicate that the policyholder (in the French text, 'preneur d'assurance') is the person who originally took out the insurance. Thus under a life policy provided by an employer to an employee, the policyholder would be the employer, the insured would be the employee and the beneficiary would be the person nominated by the employee to receive the policy proceeds. For most types of insurance, the policyholder, insured and beneficiary will be the same person.

### Actions by insurers

An insurer must usually sue a policyholder, insured or beneficiary in the contracting state in which he or she (the defendant) is domiciled (art 11). The rules for determining corporate domicile have been considered above.[90] To determine whether or not an *individual* is domiciled in a contracting state the law of that state must be applied.[91] English law[92] provides that, for these purposes, an individual is domiciled in the United Kingdom if he or she is resident there and the nature and circumstances of that residence indicate that the individual has a substantial connection with the UK. The required degree of connection will be rebuttably presumed to exist if the individual has been resident in the UK for the last three months.

There are three instances when the insurer may bring proceedings in a state other than the one in which the policyholder, insured or beneficiary is domiciled.

---

[89] Jenard (OJ 1979 C59/1 at p 31) and Schlosser (OJ 1979 C59/71 at p 117, para 152).
[90] See p 98 and pp 104–5.
[91] Article 52.
[92] Civil Jurisdiction and Judgments Act 1982, s 41.

First, where the insurer is making a counterclaim it may do so in the court where the original claim is pending (art 11, second paragraph). In practice this is unlikely to be of much benefit to insurers as the original proceedings will usually have been brought in the courts of the contracting state where the insured is domiciled.

Secondly, if the insurer has been sued in a direct action by a third party it may join the policyholder, insured or beneficiary in those proceedings if the law governing the direct action permits such joinder (art 10 third paragraph and art 11 first paragraph).

Thirdly, if the claim arises out of the operations of the defendant's branch, agency or other establishment in a different contracting state, the defendant may be sued in that contracting state (arts 7 and 5(5)).

> Example: A French company pays its insurance premiums out of its branch office in Belgium. Insufficient premium is paid. The insurer may sue the insured in Belgium.

### Actions against insurers

When the *insurer* is being sued in a matter relating to insurance, the plaintiff has a wider choice of fora. This is so whether the plaintiff is the insured, the policyholder or a beneficiary, or (where such actions are possible[93]) a third party bringing a direct action.[94] The courts in which proceedings may be brought are as follows:

First, the courts of the contracting state in which the insurer is domiciled (art 8(1)).[95] So, for example, a French insured could sue their English insurer in England.

Secondly, the courts for the place where the *policyholder* is domiciled, if this is in another contracting state (art 8(2)).[96] Thus a policyholder who is domiciled in a contracting state may sue an insurer in the state of the policyholder's own domicile. An insured who is not the policyholder may rely on this provision to found

---

[93.] Direct actions are permitted in, for example, Belgium and Spain. In England they are permitted only in limited circumstances, notably under the Third Parties (Rights Against Insurers) Act 1930 and ss 151 and 152 of the Road Traffic Act 1988.
[94.] Article 10, second paragraph.
[95.] As amended by the Luxembourg Convention.
[96.] As amended by the Luxembourg Convention.

jurisdiction but it remains the domicile of the policyholder and not that of the insured or beneficiary which determines the courts having jurisdiction.[97]

Thirdly, where the insurer is a co-insurer, the courts of a contracting state in which proceedings are brought against the leading insurer (art 8(3)).[98]

> Example: An insurance contract is led by a London company and the following market is in Germany. The insured could sue the leading insurer in England and the following insurers in Germany pursuant to art 8(1), but they could if they preferred sue all the insurers in England pursuant to art 8(3). (Article 8(3) would not permit the insured to sue the leading insurer in Germany.)

Fourthly, in disputes arising out of the operations of the insurer's branch, agency or other establishment, the courts for the place where the establishment is situated (arts 5(5) and 7).

> Example: The Belgian branch of a French insurance company provides cover to an insured in the Netherlands. The branch refuses to pay a claim. The insured may sue the insurer in Belgium.

The Convention's jurisdiction rules do not usually apply where the defendant is not domiciled in a contracting state[99] but there is an important exception to this. Article 8 paragraph 2[100] provides that where an insurer is not domiciled in a contracting state but the dispute arises out of the operations of its branch, agency or other establishment[101] in a contracting state, the insurer will be deemed to be domiciled in that contracting state for the purposes of the Convention.

> Example: The English branch of a New York insurer provides cover to a French company. A dispute arises out of the operations of the branch. The insurer would be deemed to be domiciled in England and could be sued there pursuant to arts 5(5) or 8(2).[102]

Fifthly, in respect of liability insurance or insurance of

---

97. Report by Jenard, OJ 1979 C59/1 at p 31.
98. As amended by the Luxembourg Convention.
99. See pp 98 and 126–7.
100. As amended by the Luxembourg Convention.
101. As to the meaning of 'branch, agency or other establishment' see pp 109–10.
102. Article 5(5) identifies only the contracting state in which the proceedings may be brought, whilst art 8(1) also specifies the courts within that state which are to have jurisdiction. The effect of these Articles may thus be slightly different.

immovable property, the courts for the place where the harmful event occurred (art 9).

This provision also applies if movable and immovable property are covered by the same policy and both are adversely affected by the same contingency. The meaning of 'the place where the harmful event occurred' is discussed above[103] in the context of tort claims brought under the general jurisdiction rules.

> Example: A holiday home and its contents in Italy are insured by a French insurer. The house is damaged by a windstorm. The insured may bring proceedings in Italy.

Finally, in respect of liability insurance, the insurer may be joined in proceedings brought by the injured party against the insured (art 10 first paragraph).[104]

> Example: A road accident victim sues the driver in a contracting state. That court's law allows the joinder of insurers as third parties. The insurer could be enjoined in the proceedings.

## Jurisdiction by submission

Article 18 of the Convention provides that if a plaintiff brings proceedings in a court in a contracting state and the defendant enters an appearance, the court will have jurisdiction even if under the other rules of the Convention it would not have done. This applies in both insurance and reinsurance cases. The only exception to the rule is where the defendant's appearance was made solely to contest the court's jurisdiction. Whether an appearance oversteps this point is a matter for each court's procedural rules to determine.[105]

> Example: A reinsurer starts proceedings against its reinsured in the English courts when, under the jurisdictional rules, only the French courts have jurisdiction. The reinsured acknowledges service of the writ and serves a defence on the merits of the claim. The English courts would have jurisdiction to hear the case pursuant to art 18.

This rule constitutes a serious risk for defendants, as they may

---

103. See pp 108–9.
104. The third party jurisdictions specified in Art 10 are not applicable in Germany or Austria (Protocol to the Convention, Art V (as amended)).
105. Case 150/80 *Elefanten Schuh GmbH v Pierre Jacqmain* [1981] ECR 1671.

inadvertently commit themselves to defending in a forum which is unfavourable to them by, for example, entering a holding defence while they are considering jurisdictional or other issues, or even by instructing lawyers to accept service of proceedings without reserving the right to challenge jurisdiction.

The wording of art 18 indicates that it overrides the Convention's provisions relating to jurisdiction agreements.

# Jurisdiction agreements

The parties to a contract may agree between themselves which court is to have jurisdiction. Whether their choice will be effective to override the Convention's usual allocation of jurisdiction will depend largely on whether the contract is one of reinsurance or direct insurance. In reinsurance contracts the parties are given wide freedom to make a choice of jurisdiction whereas in direct insurance their freedom is very limited.

## General rules on jurisdiction agreements (reinsurance)

The general provisions on jurisdiction agreements are set out in art 17.[106] It appears[107] that it is the general provisions, rather than the special insurance provisions (discussed below), which apply in reinsurance cases.

A jurisdiction agreement is not valid unless it is (i) in writing or evidenced in writing, or (ii) in a form which accords with practices which the parties have established between themselves, or (iii) in accordance with a widely-known and regularly observed practice in international reinsurance contracts of which the parties were, or ought to have been, aware. The Court of Justice has held that contracting states cannot impose additional formal requirements, for example that jurisdiction agreements must be in a particular language.[108] Jurisdiction agreements in reinsurance contracts will usually be made or evidenced in writing, in the form of a

---

106. Amended by the Luxembourg and San Sebastián Conventions.
107. See pp 103–4.
108. Case 150/80 *Elefanten Schuh GmbH v Pierre Jacqmain* [1981] ECR 1671 at p 1688. Additional formalities are, however, required for a jurisdiction clause to be binding on a Luxembourg domiciliary (Protocol to the Convention, art I and Case 784/79 *Porta-Leasing GmbH v Prestige International SA* [1980] ECR 1517).

jurisdiction clause in the policy. In cases where no policy has been drawn up, it *may* be sufficient if the plaintiff can clearly demonstrate that there was a consensus between the parties.

The effect of a jurisdiction agreement depends on whether or not any of the parties to it is domiciled in a contracting state. *Where one or more of the parties is domiciled in a contracting state* then if the courts chosen by the parties are in a contracting state the chosen courts will have exclusive jurisdiction (in other words, only those courts will have jurisdiction: courts in other contracting states must decline to hear the dispute).

> Example: A German company agrees to provide reinsurance to a New York company. The reinsurance contract stipulates that the English courts have exclusive jurisdiction. The English courts would have jurisdiction to hear claims brought by either party: the courts of other contracting states would not have jurisdiction.

It is not clear from the Convention whether an agreement to confer non-exclusive jurisdiction should, despite its wording, be treated as conferring exclusive jurisdiction. (A non-exclusive jurisdiction clause is one which gives the parties the right to bring proceedings in a particular forum without prohibiting them, should they prefer, from suing in any other forum which would otherwise have jurisdiction.) The English courts have given effect to non-exclusive jurisdiction agreements.[109]

Where the jurisdiction agreement was concluded for the benefit of only one of the parties, that party is not limited by the jurisdiction agreement and may bring proceedings in any other court which has jurisdiction under the Convention. Unfortunately the Convention provides no guidance for determining which of the parties was intended to benefit from the jurisdiction agreement. The Court of Justice has held that the fact that the chosen courts are in the state where one of the parties is domiciled is not in itself sufficient to show that the agreement was concluded for that party's benefit.[110] The effect of this provision is thus unclear.

If the courts chosen by the parties are not in a contracting state then a court faced with the agreement would follow its own rules

---

109. *Kurz v Stella Musical Veranstaltungs GmbH* [1992] Ch 196, approved in *Gamlestaden plc v Casa de Suecia SA and Hans Thulin* [1994] 1 Lloyd's Rep 433 at p 444. However in *Continental Bank NA v Aeakos Compania Naviera SA* [1994] 1 Lloyd's Rep 505 (CA) at p 509 Steyn LJ declined to express a view on the correctness of the *Kurz* decision.

110. Case 22/85 *Rudolf Anterist v Crédit Lyonnais* [1986] ECR 1951 at pp 1963–4.

to determine whether or not the agreement is valid. If it is found to be invalid then the Convention's jurisdiction rules will apply.[111]

*Where none of the parties to the jurisdiction agreement is domiciled in a contracting state* the Convention does not determine which courts have jurisdiction. The courts of contracting states must ascertain whether they have jurisdiction by applying their own rules. However, to remove the risk of irreconcilable judgments being handed down by the courts of different contracting states, article 17 provides a rule of priority whereby the courts of contracting states which are not nominated in the jurisdiction agreement cannot accept jurisdiction unless the courts of the contracting state which are nominated have declined jurisdiction.

### *Jurisdiction agreements in insurance matters*

The rules which apply to jurisdiction agreements in matters relating to direct insurance are set out in arts 12[112] and 12a[113]. In such cases jurisdiction agreements are generally not effective. This prevents insurers from using their superior bargaining strength to impose an unfavourable choice of forum on their insureds. A jurisdiction agreement will be effective to confer exclusive jurisdiction if, and only if, one or more of the following five requirements is satisfied:

First, the agreement was entered into after the dispute arose (art 12(1)). This provision will be little used, as once a dispute arises the insurer will be unlikely to be able to persuade the insured to agree to a choice of courts other than those of the state in which the insured is domiciled.

Secondly, the agreement allows the policyholder, insured or beneficiary to bring proceedings in courts other than those indicated in the Convention's insurance jurisdiction rules discussed above (art 12(2)). As art 12's objective is to protect the weaker parties in insurance transactions, this provision should be interpreted as widening the policyholder, insured or beneficiary's[114] choice of forum, but not the insurer's. It would seem that

---

111. Schlosser report, OJ 1979 C59/71 at p 124, para 176(a).
112. Amended by the Luxembourg Convention.
113. Inserted by the Luxembourg Convention.
114. An insured may rely on a jurisdiction agreement even if he was not a party to it: Case 201/82 *Gerling Konzern Speziale Kreditversicherungs-AG v Amministrazione del Tesoro dello Stato* [1983] ECR 2503 at p 2517.

the jurisdiction conferred by the agreement must therefore be non-exclusive *vis-à-vis* the insured.

> Example: An insurer and insured enter into an insurance contract which contains a jurisdiction clause in favour of the English courts. The other provisions of Title II Section 3 of the Convention do not grant jurisdiction to the English court. The insured could, if he or she wished, rely on the jurisdiction agreement to bring proceedings in England. The insurer could not rely on the jurisdiction agreement.

Thirdly, the agreement is concluded between a policyholder and an insurer, both of whom are at the time of the conclusion of the contract domiciled[115] or habitually resident in the same contracting state, and has the effect of conferring jurisdiction on the courts of that state even if the harmful event were to occur abroad. Such an agreement must not be contrary to the law of that state (art 12(3)).[116] (The words 'at the time of the conclusion of the contract' and 'or habitually resident', which were inserted by the Luxembourg Convention, were mistakenly omitted from the English texts of the consolidated Convention published in the Official Journal.[117] As a result, many published versions of the Convention, including the one annexed to the Civil Jurisdiction and Judgments Act 1982 (as amended),[118] are erroneous.)

This provision permits the parties to agree that any disputes must be brought in the courts of the contracting state in which they were domiciled or habitually resident, provided that such an agreement is allowed by the law of that state. Because the chosen courts will then have exclusive jurisdiction either party would be precluded from bringing proceedings in other fora which would otherwise have been available under the Convention. Like the rest of the Convention, this provision applies only where the case has an international element.[119]

---

115. This may include the deemed domicile of an insurer who is not domiciled in a contracting state, pursuant to the second paragraph of art 8 (see p 114).
116. Amended by the Luxembourg Convention.
117. OJ 1978 L304/77 (Luxembourg Convention), OJ 1983 C97/1 (Greek accession convention), OJ 1990 C189/1 (San Sebastián Convention). These versions of the text are not legally binding.
118. This has no legal consequence as s 2 of the Act provides that it is the Convention itself which has the force of law in the United Kingdom: the text annexed to the Act is solely for 'convenience of reference'.
119. See p 98.

Example 1: A life assurance contract entered into between a French-domiciled insurer and a French-domiciled policyholder names a Belgian domiciliary as the assured. The contract stipulates French jurisdiction. It is likely that the contract has the requisite international element and the Convention therefore applies. Subject to the jurisdiction agreement being effective under French law the insurer, policyholder and assured could sue only in the French courts.

Example 2: An English-domiciled insurer provides cover to an English-domiciled insured. The contract stipulates English jurisdiction. The insured subsequently becomes domiciled in New York. The English courts would have exclusive jurisdiction.

Fourthly, the agreement is concluded with a policyholder who is not domiciled in a contracting state, except in so far as the insurance is compulsory or relates to immovable property in a contracting state (art 12(4)[120]).

If the policyholder is not domiciled in a contracting state the parties may make a free choice of forum unless the insurance is of a kind which is compulsory[121] or it relates to immovable property in a contracting state. This provision is important to the United Kingdom since it is common for domiciliaries of non-contracting states to provide for English jurisdiction in their contracts.

Example: A New York company takes out product liability insurance. The contract contains an English jurisdiction clause. The English courts would have exclusive jurisdiction.

Fifthly, the agreement relates to a contract of insurance in so far as it covers certain large commercial risks (art 12(5)[122]). Where the insurance relates to certain large commercial risks the parties are presumed not to require protection and are free to choose their forum. The English Court of Appeal (declining to interpret the words 'in so far as' literally) has held that freedom of choice under this provision is available only if the contract relates *exclusively* to such risks.[123] These risks, which are listed in art 12a, are as follows:

(a) Loss of or damage to sea-going ships, off-shore installations or aircraft, arising from perils which relate to their use for

120. Inserted by the Luxembourg Convention.     121. See p 156.
122. Inserted by the Luxembourg Convention.
123. *John Robert Charman and Mark E. Brockbank v WOC Offshore BV* [1993] 2 Lloyd's Rep 551 at p 558.

commercial purposes.[124] 'Sea-going ships' has a broad meaning, covering floating apparatus which cannot move under its own power and all vessels which are intended to travel on the sea.[125]

(b) Loss of or damage to goods in transit where the transit consists of or includes carriage by such ships or aircraft.[126] Article 12a does not, however, grant freedom of choice where the insured risk is loss of or damage to passengers' baggage, as in such instances the insured is likely to have very little bargaining power.

(c) Liability arising out of the use or operation of ships, installations or aircraft. Article 12a does not grant freedom of choice where the insured risk is liability for bodily injury to passengers or loss of or damage to passengers' baggage. In relation to aircraft, the liberal regime does not apply if the law of the contracting state in which the aircraft is registered prohibits agreements on jurisdiction regarding the insurance of such risks:[127] this is intended to leave the contracting states free to provide protection for the policyholder and the victim if they consider it appropriate.[128]

(d) Liability for loss or damage caused by goods in transit described in point (b) above. The liberal regime does not apply if the insured risk is liability for bodily injury to passengers or loss of or damage to passengers' baggage.[129]

(e) Any financial loss connected with the use or operation of ships, installations or aircraft, in particular loss of freight or charter-hire.[130]

(f) Any risk or interest connected with any of those referred to in points (a) to (e) above.[131] The official report on the Luxembourg Convention cites[132], as examples of risks falling within point (f), 'shipowners' disbursements' consisting of exceptional operational costs (such as harbour dues accruing while a ship remains disabled), and insurance against 'increased value' (providing protection against loss arising from the fact that a destroyed or damaged cargo has increased in value during transit).

124. Article 12a(1)(a).
125. Report by Schlosser, OJ 1979 C59/71 at p 115, para 141.
126. Article 12a(1)(b).    127. Article 12a(2)(a).
128. Report by Schlosser, OJ 1979 C59/71 at p 115, para 144.
129. Article 12a(2)(b).    130. Article 12a(3).    131. Article 12a(4).
132. Schlosser, OJ 1979 C59/71 at pp 115–16, para 147.

The Convention does not identify the nature of the connection which is required by point (f), although the French text suggests that risks within point (f) must be accessory ('accessoirement') to risks in points (a) to (e). In the English case *Charman v WOC Offshore*[133] an insured claimed against his insurer following the loss of a mixture of sea-going and land-based equipment which had been used for the construction of a sea breakwater. The Court of Appeal held that the land-based equipment came within point (f) above. The inclusion of some trivial marine risk in a contract insuring land-based property would not, however, be effective to bring the contract within article 12a.

## Priority of proceedings

The Convention's rules sometimes grant jurisdiction to the courts of more than one contracting state. For example, a French reinsured makes negligent misrepresentations to its English reinsurer in relation to a reinsurance contract which is governed by English law. The reinsurer refuses to pay claims. In a claim by the reinsured for non-payment, the French courts could have jurisdiction under art 5(1) (place of performance of contractual obligation) and the English courts could have jurisdiction under art 2 (defendant's domicile). In a claim by the reinsurer for misrepresentation the French courts could have jurisdiction under art 2 and the English courts could have jurisdiction under art 5(1) or perhaps art 5(3) (place of the tort). Clearly, if proceedings concerning the same subject matter were allowed to proceed in more than one jurisdiction, there would be a serious risk that conflicting judgments would be given by the different courts. This would be contrary to the Convention's main aim of ensuring that the judgments of one contracting state's courts would be freely enforceable in the other contracting states.

The Convention contains three articles (arts 21 to 23) which are intended to prevent this situation from arising. Article 21 applies to proceedings involving the same cause of action and between the same parties. Article 22 applies where the actions are merely 'related'. Article 23 is unlikely to be relevant to insurance or reinsurance disputes and is not considered here.

---

133. *John Robert Charman and Mark E. Brockbank v WOC Offshore BV* [1993] 2 Lloyd's Rep 551.

## Proceedings involving the same cause of action and between the same parties

Article 21[134] applies if proceedings involving the same cause of action and between the same parties are brought in the courts of different contracting states. The English court has held,[135] in the context of reinsurance, that a claim for a declaration of avoidance involves the same cause of action as a claim for payment under the policy. In *The Maciej Rataj* the Court of Appeal[136] and the Court of Justice[137] took the same approach in the context of an application for a declaration of non-liability under a charterparty.

The Article requires any court other than the one which was first 'seised' (see below) automatically to stay its proceedings until the court which was first seised has established whether or not it has jurisdiction.[138] If the court first seised finds that it has jurisdiction, the courts which were subsequently seised must then decline jurisdiction.

> Example 1: A French reinsured makes a claim under a contract of reinsurance. The English reinsurer refuses to pay and a dispute arises. The reinsured starts proceedings in the French courts. The reinsurer subsequently starts proceedings in England, claiming a declaration of non-liability. The English proceedings cannot continue unless and until the French courts decide that they do not have jurisdiction.

> Example 2: The same dispute arises as in example 1. The reinsurer anticipates that the reinsured is likely to sue in France, but considers that England would be a more attractive forum. It pre-empts the reinsured by starting proceedings in England, claiming a declaration. The reinsured subsequently sues in France. If the English court finds that it has jurisdiction then the French courts must decline jurisdiction.

As these examples illustrate, a would-be defendant may be advantaged by making a 'pre-emptive strike' in its preferred jurisdiction, thereby preventing proceedings from being brought

---

134. Amended by the San Sebastián Convention.
135. *Overseas Union Insurance Ltd v New Hampshire Insurance Co* [1992] 1 Lloyd's Rep 218.
136. [1992] 2 Lloyd's Rep 552.
137. Case C-406/92 *sub. nom. The Tatry* [1994] ECR I-5439 at pp 5475–6.
138. See Case C-351/89 *Overseas Union Insurance Limited v New Hampshire Insurance Co* [1991] ECR I-3317 at pp 3349–51.

against it in a less favourable court. The pre-emptive strike is therefore likely to be increasingly used in international reinsurance litigation.[139]

A court is 'seised' when its proceedings become 'definitively pending'.[140] When this occurs is a matter for the relevant court's procedural law to determine. In most contracting states the court is seised when the proceedings are served on the defendant.[141] Initially it appeared[142] that the English courts were seised at an earlier stage of proceedings, namely on the issuance of the writ. This would have given an advantage to litigants who wished to make a pre-emptive strike in the English courts, as their preferred courts could be seised more quickly than those of other contracting states. However the Court of Appeal has now held[143] that under English law also it is the service of the writ which seises the court.

The expression 'the same cause of action and between the same parties' was considered by the Court of Justice in *The Maciej Rataj*. The Court held[144] that two actions will fall within this provision only in so far as the parties to them are identical. To the extent that the parties before it are not involved in proceedings in the court which was first seised, the court which is second seised may still continue to hear proceedings.

> Example: Reinsurer A starts proceedings in England against the reinsured, claiming a declaration of non-liability. The reinsured subsequently sues reinsurers A, B and C in France in respect of their failure to pay a claim. The French court must stay the reinsured's proceedings against A (unless and until the English court decides that it does not have jurisdiction), but it could continue to hear the claims against B and C.

The fragmentation of cases in this way of course increases the scope for conflicting judgments and may involve considerable

---

139. It is likely to be rarely used in direct insurance as in such cases the Convention generally requires the insurer to sue the insured in the courts of the contracting state in which the insured is domiciled: see pp 112–13.

140. Case 129/83 *Siegfried Zelger v Sebastiano Salinitri (No 2)* [1984] ECR 2397 at p 2408.

141. Ibid at p 2407. See also O'Malley and Layton, *European Civil Practice* (Sweet & Maxwell, 1989), p 634.

142. *Kloeckner & Co AG v Gatoil Overseas Inc* [1990] 1 Lloyd's Rep 177 at p 204.

143. *Dresser UK Ltd v Falcongate Freight Management Ltd* [1991] 2 Lloyd's Rep 557; *Neste Chemicals SA v DK Line SA, The Sargasso* [1994] 2 Lloyd's Rep 6.

144. Case C-406/92 [1994] ECR I-5439 at pp 5473–4.

extra expenditure of costs and effort. The Court of Justice therefore drew attention[145] to the fact that these difficulties could be mitigated by the court which was second seised exercising its discretion to stay the case under art 22 (see below).

## Proceedings involving related actions

Article 22 applies if related actions are brought in the courts of different contracting states. In such circumstances any court other than the court first seised *may*, while the actions are pending at first instance, stay its proceedings. A court other than the court first seised may also (on the application of one of the parties) decline jurisdiction if the court first seised has jurisdiction over both actions and the latter court's law would permit the actions to be consolidated. Actions are 'related' where they are so closely connected that it is expedient to hear and determine them together to avoid the risk of irreconcilable judgments.[146]

In Case C-406/92 *The Maciej Rataj* the Court of Justice[147] gave art 22 a broad interpretation, holding that it is satisfied whenever there is a risk that the two courts' judgments would be contradictory or conflicting even if the judgments could be separately enforced and their legal consequences would not be mutually exclusive. The Court also held that this article applies where a number of plaintiffs bring separate actions against the same defendant in respect of separate but identical contracts. Thus if two reinsureds commenced separate actions in different fora against a single reinsurer in respect of an unpaid claim, the court which was second seised could stay its proceedings (or, on the reinsurer's request, decline jurisdiction if the actions could be consolidated in the court which was first seised).

However, the mere fact that one court might address some issues of fact or law which would also be addressed by the other court does not necessarily bring the actions within art 22. The English Court of Appeal has held[148] that for the article to apply the common issues must be 'primary' ones, in the sense that it is essential for the court to decide them in order to reach its judgment in the particular case.

---

145. Ibid at p 5474.
146. Article 22, third paragraph.
147. [1994] ECR I-5439 at pp 5478–80.
148. *Sarrio SA v Kuwait Investment Authority*, 12 August 1996 (unreported).

## Where the defendant is not domiciled in a contracting state or the alternative forum is in a non-contracting state

If the defendant is not domiciled in a contracting state then the court follows its own rules rather than those elaborated in the Convention to determine whether it has jurisdiction,[149] subject to the proviso that it may not accept jurisdiction if this would contravene the principles in arts 21 to 23. The English rules of court permit the court to decline jurisdiction if it considers that England is not the most appropriate forum which is available to hear the dispute (the principle of *forum non conveniens*).[150]

There has been considerable debate about whether courts should apply their own rules or those of the Convention where proceedings are contemplated in a contracting state and a non-contracting state rather than two contracting states.

In *S&W Berisford Plc v New Hampshire Insurance Co*[151] an American insured sued its American insurer in England (on the basis that the insurer was deemed, pursuant to art 8, to be domiciled there). The insurer argued that the Convention did not apply and that the court should apply its own rules and stay proceedings on the ground that England was not the most appropriate forum. Hobhouse J held that where a defendant was regarded as domiciled in a contracting state the court was bound to follow the Convention's jurisdiction rules. Proceedings had been brought in England pursuant to those rules and the court had no residual power to grant a stay. This decision was followed in *Arkwright Mutual Insurance Co v Bryanston Insurance Co Ltd.*[152] Reinsurers brought proceedings in New York for a declaration of non-liability. The reinsureds sued the reinsurers in England. Potter J held that the English court was obliged to accept jurisdiction pursuant to the Convention as arts 21 and 22 did not permit the court to stay proceedings or decline jurisdiction except in favour of the courts of another contracting state.

However these decisions were overruled by the Court of Appeal in *In re Harrods (Buenos Aires) Ltd.*[153] The Court of Appeal there held that the Convention applies only if there is a conflict with the

149. Article 4.
150. *Sarrio SA v Kuwait Investment Authority* [1996] 1 Lloyd's Rep 650 (Mance J) and 12 August 1996 (unreported) (CA).
151. [1990] 2 QB 631, [1990] 1 Lloyd's Rep 454.
152. [1990] 2 QB 649, [1990] 2 Lloyd's Rep 70.
153. [1992] Ch 72.

courts of another contracting state. Since the alternative forum (Argentina) was not in a contracting state the court applied English procedural rules, and stayed the claim on the grounds that England was not the most appropriate forum. The question whether this was the correct approach was referred to the Court of Justice but the case was settled before the hearing.

Although *Harrods* has been approved and followed in a number of subsequent English cases[154] the decision is controversial since it is arguable[155] that the Court of Appeal took too restrictive a view of the Convention's effect. In *The Nile Rhapsody*[156] Neill LJ referred to the substantial amount of academic and other criticism of the decision and stated that the extent to which the English court retained the discretion to stay proceedings on *forum non conveniens* grounds was an important one which at some stage would have to be determined by the European Court of Justice. However, he decided not to refer the question to the Court on that occasion. In *The ERAS EIL actions*[157] Potter J acknowledged that there were 'detailed and interesting' arguments both in favour of and against the *Harrods* decision but declared himself bound by it. It is to be hoped that it will not be long before the Court of Justice has the occasion to resolve this important issue.

---

154. Including *Hamed el Chiaty & Co v The Thomas Cook Group Ltd, The Nile Rhapsody* [1994] 1 Lloyd's Rep 382 (CA); *The ERAS EIL actions* [1995] 1 Lloyd's Rep 64 at pp 76–7; *Sarrio SA v Kuwait Investment Authority*, 12 August 1996 (unreported) (CA). See also *Owens Bank Ltd v Bracco* [1992] 2 AC 443 (CA).

155. See, for example, Cheshire and North, *Private International Law* 12th edn (Butterworths, 1992), at pp 333–4.

156. *Hamed el Chiaty & Co v The Thomas Cook Group Ltd* [1994] 1 Lloyd's Rep 382 at pp 391–2.

157. [1995] 1 Lloyd's Rep 64 at p 77.

# CHAPTER SIX

# Choice of law

## Introduction

Which law applies to a contract can determine the success or failure of a claim. For example, a party might be liable under English law for breach of contract whilst there might be no breach or even no contract under French law.

Until the 1980s the member states had no harmonised approach to identifying the applicable law, although the member states' approaches sometimes shared similar features such as the principle that the parties to a contract should in some circumstances be permitted to choose the law applicable to it. The first step towards harmonisation was taken in 1967 when, with the successful completion of the Brussels Convention[1] in sight, the governments of Belgium and the Netherlands invited the Commission to collaborate in the creation of a code of conflict of laws rules for the entire Community. It was thought that the harmonisation of at least some fields of private international law would serve a number of purposes, in particular (i) it would increase legal certainty, since it would be easier for contracting parties to determine which law would govern their contract, (ii) it would prevent 'forum shopping' (i.e., parties selecting a forum to hear disputes on the basis that the chosen forum would apply a more advantageous law than other fora), and (iii) it would therefore be likely to encourage the free movement of goods, persons and capital among the member states. The proposed harmonisation was not directly based on any provision of the EEC Treaty but was regarded as 'a natural sequel' to the Brussels Convention.[2]

[1.] See chapter 5.
[2.] Report on the Rome Convention by Giuliano and Lagarde, OJ 1980 C282/1 at p 5.

The Commission appointed a group of experts to work on the harmonisation, and the Convention on the Law Applicable to Contractual Obligations[3] (hereafter 'the Rome Convention' or 'the Convention') was finally opened for signature on 19 June 1980. The Convention provides, in essence, that a contract is governed by whichever law the parties choose. It is now in force in Belgium, Denmark, France, Germany, Greece[4], Ireland, Italy, Luxembourg, the Netherlands, Portugal[5], Spain[6] and the United Kingdom (as to the dates of ratification and entry into force see below). Austria, Finland and Sweden agreed[7] to accede to the Convention and the convention for their accession was signed in Brussels on 29 November 1996.

The Convention does not apply to contracts of direct insurance if the insured risks are situated in the EC. The conflicts rules applying to such contracts were later laid down in two EC directives, the Second Non-Life Directive[8] (which applies to non-life risks[9] situated in the EC) and the Second Life Directive[10] (which applies to contracts insuring life risks[11] situated in the EC). Initially both of these Directives took a less liberal approach to jurisdiction than the Convention, restricting the parties' freedom of choice in order to prevent insurers from imposing an unfavourable choice of law on their policyholders. However, the rules in the Second Non-Life Directive have since been modified by the Third Non-Life Directive to give the parties freedom of choice in more instances.

3. OJ 1980 L266/1 (corrigenda to which are at OJ 1983 L58/14).
4. Greece acceded to the Rome Convention by the Luxembourg Convention of 10 April 1984, OJ 1984 L146/1.
5. Portugal and Spain acceded to the Rome Convention by the Funchal Convention of 18 May 1992, OJ 1992 L333/1.
6. See note 5 above.
7. By article 4 of the Act concerning their accession to the Community, OJ 1994 C241/21.
8. OJ 1988 L172/1.
9. I.e., those listed in the Annex to the First Non-Life Directive (OJ 1973 L228/17), namely: accident, sickness, land vehicles (other than railway rolling stock), railway rolling stock, aircraft, ships (sea, lake and river and canal vessels), goods in transit (including merchandise, baggage, and all other goods), fire and natural forces, other damage to property, motor vehicle liability, aircraft liability, liability for ships, general liability, credit, suretyship, miscellaneous financial loss, legal expenses.
10. OJ 1990 L330/50.
11. I.e., those listed in the Annex to the First Life Directive (OJ 1979 L63/1), including life assurance, annuities, supplementary insurance carried on by life assurance undertakings, marriage assurance, birth assurance, permanent health insurance, tontines, capital redemption operations and management of group pension funds.

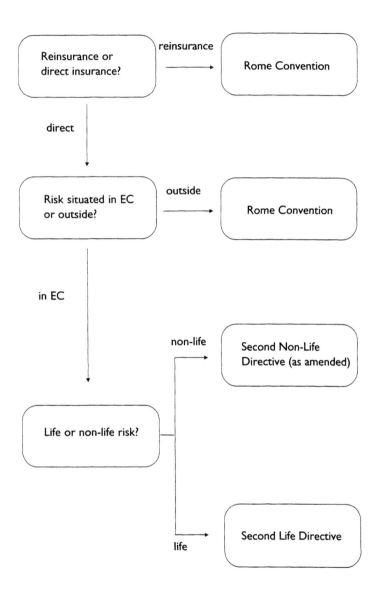

**Figure 6.1** Rome Convention or Directives?

*Note:* For implementation of the Rome Convention and the Directives in member states see Appendices 3 and 4 respectively.

## *Which contracts are covered by the Convention and which by the Directives?*

Where the contract is one of reinsurance, the courts of a contracting state will determine the applicable law in accordance with the rules in the Convention.[12] Where the contract is of direct insurance then the applicable law will be determined in accordance with the rules in the Convention if the insured risk is situated outside the EC. If the risk is situated within the EC then the rules in the Second Non-Life Directive (as amended by the Third Non-Life Directive) or the Second Life Directive, depending on the type of risk insured, will apply. These principles are illustrated in Figure 6.1 (opposite).

The Convention provides[13] that the question of where a risk is situated is to be determined by the internal law of the forum. Article 2(d) of the Second Non-Life Directive contains rules for determining which member state a risk is situated in.[14] These provide that a risk is situated as shown in Table 6.1 (overleaf).

> Example: An individual policyholder who is habitually resident in England insures a painting in New York against damage; proceedings on the contract are brought in the courts of a contracting state. The court would consider the risk to be situated in England. The applicable law would therefore be determined by reference to the Second Non-Life Directive rather than the Rome Convention.

It is not clear which of the regimes (Convention or Directives) is to be applied where a contract of direct insurance covers risks which are only partially situated in the EC, for example if one risk is situated in a member state and another risk is situated in a non-member state. One possibility is that the Directives' rules apply to the first risk and the Convention's rules apply to the second (with the possible effect that, particularly if no express choice of law was made, different laws would apply in respect of

---

12. Article 1(4).   13. Article 1(3).
14. These rules are stated (at art 2 of the Second Non-Life Directive) to be for the purposes of that Directive. English law also adopts them as the relevant 'internal law' for the purposes of art 1(3) of the Rome Convention: Contracts (Applicable Law) Act 1990 (as amended), s 2(1A). If the internal law of a member state were to contain different rules for the purposes of the Rome Convention the insurance contracts excluded from the Rome Convention and those covered by the Second Non-Life and Second Life Directives would not be co-extensive.

**Table 6.1**   Situation of risk

| Type of risk | Where the risk is considered situated |
|---|---|
| Buildings or buildings and their contents | In the member state in which the property is situated |
| Motor vehicles of any type | In the member state of registration |
| Travel or holiday risks, whatever the class of business, if the policy is of a duration of four months or less | In the member state where the policyholder took out the policy |
| All other instances | In the member state where the policyholder has his or her habitual residence (if the policyholder is an individual[15]) or in the member state where the policyholder's establishment, to which the contract relates, is situated (if the policyholder is a legal person) |

each risk). This solution is difficult to extend to the situation where the same risk is situated both within and outside the EC (for example, jewellery owned by an individual who is habitually resident in London and New York): it is arguable[16] that in this case the Directive would apply to the entire contract.

There is also uncertainty about how the court should identify 'the policyholder's establishment, to which the contract relates' and this may cause difficulties if a policyholder insures its establishments in several countries under a single contract.

### States with more than one legal system

For the purposes of identifying the applicable law under the Convention and the Directives, where a state contains several

---

15. The word individual is used herein to refer to a natural person.
16. On the basis that the test for exclusion from the Convention (art 1(3)) is satisfied as is the test for coverage (art 1(7)) by the Second Non-Life Directive.

territorial units each of which has its own rules of law then each territorial unit is regarded as a country for the purposes of identifying the applicable law (for example a German court may determine whether English or Scottish law applies to a contract). However, where such states are considering conflicts solely between the laws of their own territorial units they are not bound to apply the Convention's or the Directives' rules[17] (within the United Kingdom the Convention and Directives do apply in such cases[18]).

## Implementation

The dates of ratification and entry into force of the Convention in the various member states are set out in Appendix 3. The Convention does not apply to contracts made before the Convention entered into force in the relevant member state.[19] In English law the Convention is implemented by the Contracts (Applicable Law) Act 1990.[20]

The Directives have now been implemented in most of the member states[21] but in many instances the implementation was not effected until after the stipulated deadlines (the relevant implementation deadlines are identified in Appendix 4). If an individual suffers damage as a result of a member state's failure timeously to implement a Directive's provisions in national law the individual may, if certain conditions are satisfied,[22] be able to claim compensation from the state. In English law the choice of law rules in the Second Non-Life and Second Life Directives were implemented by amendments to the Insurance Companies Act 1982[23] which took effect on 1 July 1990 (Second Non-Life

---

17. Rome Convention, art 19. Second Non-Life Directive, art 7(1)(i). Second Life Directive, art 4(3).
18. Contracts (Applicable Law) Act 1990, s 2(3) (in relation to the Rome Convention); Insurance Companies Act 1982, Sched 3A, Pt I, para 4(2) (in relation to the Second Non-Life Directive); Insurance Companies Act 1982, Sched 3A, Pt II, para 9(2) (in relation to the Second Life Directive).
19. Article 17.   20. As amended.   21. The notable exception being Greece.
22. As to which see Joined Cases C-6/90 and C-9/90 *Francovich v Italian Republic* [1991] ECR I-5357; Joined Cases C-46/93 and C-48/93 *Brasserie du Pêcheur SA v Germany, R v Secretary of State for Transport, ex parte Factortame Ltd (No. 3)* [1996] 1 CMLR 889, [1996] 1 All ER (EC) 301.
23. The rules are contained in s 94B and Sched 3A of the Act. The choice of law rules applicable to contracts of insurance made by friendly societies are contained in the Friendly Societies Act 1992 (as amended).

Directive) and 20 May 1993 (Second Life Directive) (the English courts will continue to apply the old common law rules to contracts entered into before these dates).

## The EEA Agreement – applicability of the Directives in EFTA states

By the Final Act of 2 May 1992[24] the then twelve EC member states and seven EFTA states (Austria, Finland, Iceland, Liechtenstein, Norway, Sweden and Switzerland) adopted the text of the European Economic Area Agreement[25] which provided[26] for the extension to the EFTA states of many EC measures, including all of the insurance directives referred to in this chapter. Switzerland was unable to ratify the Agreement and was subsequently removed from it[27] (initially Liechtenstein was also unable to ratify the Agreement but it was permitted to do so at a later date).[28]

A draft of the EEA Agreement envisaged the creation of an EEA Court of Justice which would be staffed by judges from the European Court of Justice and each of the EFTA states but this proposal was abandoned following an opinion[29] from the European Court of Justice which declared it to be incompatible with the EC Treaty. Instead, an EFTA court was created[30] in Geneva with jurisdiction to give advisory rulings on references from EFTA states. (Although the EEA Agreement still contains provisions[31] whereby EFTA states may in certain circumstances request an advisory ruling from the European Court of Justice they have never been used.) To ensure consistency of interpretation, the EFTA Court is bound by decisions of the European Court of

---

24. OJ 1994 L1/523.    25. OJ 1994 L1/3.

26. At arts 7(b) and 36(2) and Annex IX. The Third Non-Life Directive was included in Annex IX by Annex 9 of the EEA Joint Committee Decision of 21.3.94, OJ 1994 L160/1 (this Decision excluded the application of the Directive to Finland, but Finland later accepted the Directive when it acceded to the EC: OJ 1995 L1/145).

27. By the Final Act of 17.3.93, OJ 1994 L1/598. The Agreement between the EC and the Swiss Confederation on non-life insurance (OJ 1991 L205/1) does not contain any provisions relating to applicable law.

28. EEA Council Decision of 10.3.95, OJ 1995 L86/58. Annex 6 of the Decision laid down a timetable for Liechtenstein's implementation of the Third Non-Life Directive.

29. [1991] ECR I-6079.

30. By an agreement of 2.5.92, OJ 1944 L344/1 (hereafter the 'EFTA Court Agreement').

31. Arts 107, 111(3) and Protocol 34.

Justice given prior to the signature of the EEA Agreement and must take due account of decisions given thereafter[32] and the EEA Joint Committee is charged with the duty of keeping the development of the case law under constant review.[33] The significance of the EFTA Court has considerably diminished with the accession of Austria, Finland and Sweden to the EC.

## The Rome Convention

The Convention is not strictly a Community instrument in that it was not directly derived from any provision of the EEC Treaty but was freely concluded between the contracting states. However, in a Joint Declaration[34] annexed to the Convention the contracting states expressed the wish that any state which joins the Community should accede to the Convention.

The Convention will lapse on 1 April 2001. Thereafter it will be tacitly renewed every five years although any contracting state may denounce it by giving notice, such denunciation having effect only in relation to that state.[35] The Convention leaves open the possibility of further harmonisation of choice of law matters by stipulating that any acts of the institutions of the EC containing choice of law rules, or any national laws implementing such acts, will take precedence over the Convention.[36] In addition, the Convention provides that it shall not prejudice the application of other international conventions to which a contracting state is, or becomes, a party.[37]

### Interpretation

The Convention was originally drawn up in seven languages (Danish, Dutch, English, French, German, Irish and Italian). Greek, Portuguese and Spanish language texts were later established.[38] Each version is of equal authority.[39]

An official report[40] on the Convention (hereafter called the 'Report') was prepared by Professor Mario Giuliano of the

32. EFTA Court Agreement, art 3.   33. EEA Agreement, art 105.
34. OJ 1980 L266/14.   35. Article 30.   36. Article 20.   37. Article 21.
38. By the Luxembourg and Funchal Conventions (see notes 4 and 5 above). Finnish and Swedish are added by the convention for the accession of Austria, Finland and Sweden.
39. Article 33.   40. OJ 1980 C282/1.

University of Milan and Professor Paul Lagarde of the University of Paris I. The Report may be used as an aid to interpreting the Convention.[41]

It was recognised that the Convention might lose much of its value as a harmonising instrument if its provisions were not interpreted consistently in the various member states. Article 18 of the Convention therefore provides that 'In the interpretation and application of [the Convention's] uniform rules, regard shall be had to their international character and to the desirability of achieving uniformity in their interpretation and application'.

As the Convention did not derive from the EEC Treaty it conferred no right to refer questions of interpretation to the European Court of Justice. The Commission, however, stated[42] that this was a 'totally unacceptable' situation, and a Joint Declaration[43] annexed to the Convention declared the contracting states ready to examine the possibility of conferring jurisdiction on the Court of Justice to prevent differences of interpretation arising. In 1988 two Protocols were signed by the (then) twelve member states. The first Protocol[44] ('the Brussels Protocol') established a set of rules for referrals to the Court whilst the second Protocol[45] provided for the conferral of the necessary jurisdiction on the Court. Under the Protocols contracting states' courts of appeal and of last instance would be permitted to refer questions to the Court for a preliminary ruling where the referring court considered that this was necessary to enable it to reach judgment. The 'competent authority' of a member state could also make a referral if judgments of that state's courts conflicted with rulings of the Court of Justice or judgments of the courts of other contracting states. The Brussels Protocol also contained a Joint Declaration[46] in which the member states declared themselves ready to organise a system of exchange of information on judgments handed down pursuant to the Convention. Neither of these Protocols has yet received sufficient ratifications to enter into effect, and therefore no mechanism exists for the referral of questions to the Court of Justice or for the exchange of information on judgments.[47] It is not clear whether or when the Protocols will come into force.

---

41. See s 3(3)(a) of the Contracts (Applicable Law) Act 1990.
42. Opinion of 17.3.80, OJ 1980 L94/39 at p 40.
43. OJ 1980 L266/17.    44. OJ 1989 L48/1.
45. OJ 1989 L48/17.    46. OJ 1989 L48/8.
47. The Court currently maintains, for its internal use, a database of such national judgments as are notified to it.

## Ambit of the Convention

The Convention's rules apply whenever a court in a contracting state is required to make a choice between the laws of different countries[48] and the contract was made after the Convention's entry into force.[49] The rules apply even if the contract has no connection with the EC. For example, the English courts must follow the Convention to determine which law applies to a contract made between a Swiss reinsurer and a Norwegian reinsured (such a case might be brought in the English courts if, for example, the contract contained an English jurisdiction clause).

It has already been stated that the Convention excludes contracts of direct insurance of risks situated in the EC. There are two other exclusions which are relevant in the context of insurance and reinsurance. The first relates to the question of whether an agent is able to bind its principal to a third party.[50] The second exclusion is of arbitration and jurisdiction agreements.[51] The court will apply its own law to each of these matters.

The applicable law determines[52] matters of interpretation, performance, the consequences of breach[53] including the assessment of damages,[54] the various ways of extinguishing obligations and prescription and limitation rules, and the consequences of nullity of the contract.[55] The question of whether a contract exists or is valid must generally be determined by the law which would be applicable under the rules of the Convention.[56]

# The Convention's rules for determining the applicable law

In outline the Convention's rules are as follows. The parties are

---

48. Article 1(1).  49. Article 17.  50. Article 1(2)(f).  51. Article 1(2)(d).
52. Article 10.
53. 'within the limits of the powers conferred on the court by its procedural law' (art 10(1)(c)).
54. 'in so far as that is governed by rules of law' (art 10(1)(c)).
55. Article 22(1)(b) permits contracting states to enter a reservation in respect of the last head. The United Kingdom has entered a reservation, and has not implemented the head, because under English and Scottish law questions about the nullity of contracts 'do not form part of the law of contract, but of the law of restitution or recompense' (*per* Lord Advocate, 513 HL Official Report 1259, 12.12.89).
56. Article 8(1). Under art 8(2), the question of whether a party gave consent may sometimes be determined by a different law. Special rules relating to questions of formal validity are contained in art 9.

free to choose any law to govern their contract. If they have expressed their choice it will be upheld. If no express choice was made, the court will consider whether the parties made a choice of law without expressing it, and if so will give effect to that choice. If the court finds that the parties made no choice, it will apply the law with which the contract is objectively most closely connected, as to which the Convention provides a rebuttable presumption. Regardless of the law which is generally applicable to the contract, the court may in certain circumstances apply particular rules ('mandatory rules') of a different law. Special rules apply to protect consumers in certain circumstances. These principles are considered in more detail below.

### Applicable law where the parties have made an express choice of law

The Convention gives the parties the freedom to choose any law to govern their contract.[57] The chosen law need not be the law of an EC member state. So, for example, a choice of New York law in a contract between a German reinsurer and a French reinsured would be upheld.

The choice may be made or varied at any time. Where the choice is varied, questions of formal validity will still be determined by the law originally applicable and third party rights may not be prejudiced.[58]

### Applicable law where the parties have made a choice but not expressed it

Where the parties have not made an express choice of law the court will consider whether the parties made a choice of law which they did not express. If so, it will uphold the choice. Such a choice must be 'demonstrated with reasonable certainty by the terms of the contract or the circumstances of the case'.[59] The Report states[60] that this provision applies only if the parties have made a 'real' choice of law: it 'does not permit the court to infer a choice of law

---

[57.] Article 3(1).

[58.] Article 3(2). The Report suggests (at p 18) that if the choice of law is made or changed in the course of proceedings, the effectiveness of the choice or change is to be determined by the law of the forum.

[59.] Article 3(1).  [60.] At p 17.

that the parties might have made where they had no clear intention of making a choice'; in other words, the parties must have addressed their minds to the question.

By way of illustration of terms and circumstances which may lead the court to conclude that the parties had made a 'real' choice of law the Report cites[61] the following: (i) that the contract is in a standard form which is known to be governed by a particular system of law even though there is no express statement to this effect, such as a Lloyd's policy of marine insurance; (ii) that there has been a previous course of dealings between the same parties under contracts containing an express choice of law and the choice of law clause has been omitted in circumstances which do not indicate a deliberate change of policy; (iii) that the parties have chosen a particular forum (but any presumption that they intended the law of the forum to apply must always be subject to the other terms of the contract and all the circumstances of the case); (iv) that the contract refers to the provisions of a particular law such as specific Articles of the French Civil Code; (v) that there is an express choice of law in related transactions between the same parties; and (vi) that there is a choice of the place of arbitration in circumstances which indicate that the arbitrator should apply the law of that place.

Some of these examples seem to confuse situations where the parties have made a real choice with situations where they have not. For example, the fact that the parties have used a Lloyd's marine policy does not in reality show that they have given any thought to the question of the applicable law. Moreover, the suggestion that the law applicable to Lloyd's marine policies or any other contract should be determined, in effect, by custom appears to conflict with the Convention's aim of providing a consistent framework of rules by which to determine the applicable law.

Implied choice of law under the Convention was considered in the English case *Egon Oldendorff v Libera Corporation*.[62] In that case Japanese owners agreed to charter two vessels to a German partnership. The form of charterparty incorporated an arbitration clause providing for disputes to be resolved in London by arbitrators conversant with shipping matters. In a judgment on an interlocutory application Mance J considered that this indicated that the parties intended the arbitrators to apply English law. The

61. A p 17.    62. [1995] 2 Lloyd's Rep 64.

question was raised again as a preliminary issue before Clarke J.[63] The judge found that the arbitration clause was a strong indication of the parties' intention to choose English law. The principal reason for this decision was that it was reasonable to infer that the parties, having agreed a neutral forum, intended that forum to apply a neutral law, namely English law rather than German or Japanese law. The judge took account of further factors, such as the use of terms in negotiations which had established meanings in English maritime law, and remarked that he had taken an approach which was 'very similar' to that which applied under the pre-Convention rules. These decisions suggest that the English courts, at least, may not be averse to finding that the parties have made an implied choice of law.

### Applicable law where the parties have made no choice

Where the parties have not made a choice of law which is expressed or demonstrated with reasonable certainty by the terms of the contract or the circumstances of the case, the Convention provides that the contract is governed by the law of the country with which the contract is most closely connected.[64]

The Convention provides a rebuttable presumption as to the country with which the contract is most closely connected.[65] The presumption involves two stages. First, the court must determine which of the parties to the contract is required to give the 'performance which is characteristic of the contract' (see below). Secondly, the court must then identify the country in which (at the time of conclusion of the contract) that party's principal place of business was situated (or if under the terms of the contract the performance is to be effected through a place of business other than the principal place of business, the country in which that other place of business is situated). The presumption is that the contract is most closely connected with the law of this second country. The concept of 'characteristic performance' is not defined in the Convention. The Report explains[66] that contractual obligations typically fall into two types, the first being an obligation to pay money, the second (the characteristic performance) being the performance for which the payment is due.

Article 4(5) provides that if the characteristic performance of

---

63. [1996] 1 Lloyd's Rep 380.   64. Article 4(1).   65. Article 4(2).   66. At p 20.

the contract cannot be determined then the court must identify the country with which the contract is most closely connected without regard to the presumption. Although it might be thought that a contract of insurance involves no characteristic performance, as both parties' obligations involve the payment (or contingent payment) of money, the Report cites[67] the provision of insurance as an example of characteristic performance. This is also likely to be true of reinsurance. Article 4(5) therefore does not apply and the usual presumption will be that a contract of insurance (or reinsurance) is most closely connected with the law of the country in which the insurer (or reinsurer) has its principal place of business.

> Example: An individual purchases insurance cover for an art collection in America from an insurance company which has its principal place of business in England; the contract does not specify which of the insurer's branches is to effect performance. The contract would, in the absence of an express or implied choice of law, be presumed to be governed by English law.

Where the same risk is covered by insurers or reinsurers in several countries, this approach has the consequence that different laws may apply in respect of the same risk. This is disadvantageous to the insured and may be contrary to the Convention's aim of encouraging legal certainty. It also fails to give effect to the purpose for which the concept of 'characteristic performance' was devised, namely to 'link ... the contract to the social and economic environment of which it will form part'.[68] The court might avoid these infelicities by finding that it appears, from the circumstances as a whole, that the contract is more closely connected with a country other than the one which is indicated by the presumption, as art 4(5) permits the presumption to be disregarded in such cases.

The presumption was rebutted in a comparable situation in the English case *Bank of Baroda v Vysya Bank Limited*.[69] There Mance J considered three contracts arising in relation to a letter of credit. He applied the presumption in respect of two of the contracts, finding that English law applied in each case because the characteristic performance was to be given by a company through its office in London. However he refused to apply the presumption

---

[67.] At p 20.    [68.] Report, at p 20.    [69.] [1994] 2 Lloyd's Rep 87.

to the third contract where this would have led to that contract being governed by Indian law. The application of the presumption would, he said, have led to a 'wholly anomalous' situation whereby a single credit would have been governed by different laws as between different parties. The Convention 'was not intended to confuse legal relationships or to disrupt normal expectations' in this way and the judge therefore held that English law also applied to the third contract. The judge also took into account the fact that the 'object or focus' of the third transaction (the confirmation of the credit) was to be performed in England. This decision suggests that the English courts may continue to follow their pre-Convention approach whereby, in the absence of a choice of law, insurance contracts have been held to be governed by the law of the place where the various transactions had their 'centre of gravity'.[70] This approach would permit the courts to find that a single law, for example the law of the place where the brokers placed the risk, applies even where there are several contracts involving parties in different jurisdictions.[71] This would fulfil the objectives of the 'characteristic performance' test, but whether it will be accepted in principle by the courts of other member states, and if so how it will be applied in practice, remains to be seen.

### Possibility of different laws applying to different parts of the contract (dépeçage)

The Convention provides that part of a contract may be governed by a different law from that which governs the rest (such severance is called 'dépeçage').[72]

Dépeçage may be effected pursuant to the parties' own choice provided that the different parts of the contract can be governed

---

70. In *Cantieri Navali Riuniti SpA v NV Omne Justitia, The Stolt Marmaro* [1985] 2 Lloyd's Rep 428, the Court of Appeal decided that an insurance contract was governed by English law because of the role which the English marketplace had played in the transaction: the contract was made in London, with English leading underwriters, through brokers working in the London market, under a policy introduced by the London brokers who were accustomed to working in accordance with English law and practice.

71. However in *Crédit Lyonnais v New Hampshire Insurance Company*, 16 September 1996 (unreported), a case involving the applicable law rules of the Second Non-Life Directive, the English commercial court declined to find that policies issued to branches or subsidiaries of a multinational company were all governed by the same law: see pp 153–4.

72. Articles 3(1) and 4(1).

by different laws without giving rise to contradictions: otherwise the court must apply the law with which the contract is objectively most closely connected.[73]

The court may also effect dépeçage where the parties have not made a choice of law or have made a choice which applies only to part of the contract. The part to be severed must be independent and separable (in terms of the contract rather than the dispute) and have a closer connection with the law of another country.[74] However the court 'must have recourse to severance as seldom as possible'[75] as this power is to be used only 'by way of exception'.[76]

Dépeçage may have particular importance in reinsurance contracts, where the terms of underlying contracts are often incorporated with the intention that the contracts should be interpreted 'back to back'.

> Example: An insurance contract governed by New York law is reinsured under a contract governed generally by English law; the reinsurance contract includes the same definition-of-loss clause as the underlying contract. The court might 'by way of exception' find that the choice of English law in the reinsurance contract does not apply to this clause and construe the clause in accordance with New York law. (The parties could, if they wished, expressly state that all the clauses are to be governed by English law and so preclude such an approach.)[77]

## Mandatory rules and public policy

The Convention provides that, regardless of the law generally applicable to the contract, the court may sometimes apply certain rules (known as 'mandatory rules') of a different law. 'Mandatory rules' are those legal rules which cannot be derogated from by contract.[78] They are typically found in the fields of consumer and

---

73. Report, at p 17.   74. Ibid at p 23.   75. Ibid at p 23.   76. Article 4(1).
77. Cp the non-Convention case of *Forsikringsaktieselskapet Vesta v Butcher* [1986] 2 All ER 488.
78. Article 3(3). Mandatory rules constitute a derogation from the principle of free movement of services contained in art 59 of the EEC Treaty. It would therefore appear that a member state may designate a rule as mandatory only where this is justified on the grounds of either public policy (restrictively defined in Case 30/77 *R v Pierre Bouchereau*, [1977] ECR 1999) or 'the general good' (defined in Case 205/84 *Commission v Federal Republic of Germany*, [1986] ECR 3755 and referred to in recital 19 of the preamble to the Third Non-Life Directive, OJ 1992 L228/1). The Commission is currently preparing a publication setting out its understanding of 'the general good' in the insurance sector.

employment law and are therefore of greater relevance to direct insurance than to reinsurance. Such rules may apply in four circumstances:

First, where all the elements (excepting the parties' choice of law and any accompanying choice of jurisdiction) relevant to the situation at the time of the choice of law are connected with one country only, but the parties have chosen the law of a different country (art 3(3)). In such cases the parties' choice of law 'shall not . . . prejudice' the application of the former country's mandatory rules.

> Example: An insurance contract is effected with an English company which, in contravention of s 2 of the Insurance Companies Act 1982, is not authorised to conduct insurance business in England; the situation is connected only with England except that the contract stipulates Spanish law and gives the Spanish courts jurisdiction. The Spanish courts may give effect to the rule of English law[79] that the contract is generally unenforceable by the insurer (if this is a mandatory rule).

Secondly, where the situation[80] has a close connection with another country from that whose law is applicable (art 7(1)). In such cases the court may give effect to the former country's rules, but only in so far as the former country's law requires the rules to be applied whatever the law applicable to the contract. In deciding whether to give effect to these rules, the court must have regard to their nature and purpose and to the consequences of their application or non-application. The Report states that it is essential that there be a genuine connection between the contract as a whole and the other country: a 'merely vague connection' is insufficient. The Report gives, as an example of a genuine connection, the situation when the contract is to be performed in that other country or when one party is resident or has their main place of business in that country.[81]

The factors defining a 'close connection' and the criteria to be applied by the court are far from clear and this provision would appear to be a recipe for confusion. In view of the uncertainties surrounding the provision, various member states[82] have entered a

---

79. Financial Services Act 1986, s 132(1).
80. The word 'situation' in this provision refers to 'the contract as a whole' and not to the point in dispute: Report, at p 27.
81. Report, at p 27.
82. Germany, Ireland, Luxembourg and the United Kingdom.

reservation regarding its implementation. Such reservations are permitted by art 22(1)(a).

Thirdly, where rules of the law of the forum are mandatory irrespective of the law otherwise applicable to the contract (art 7(2)).

> Example: A contract of insurance of a risk in New York is governed by New York law; a claim is brought before a court in Belgium; the contract contains a 'claims made' provision (i.e., one which restricts the provision of cover to occurrences notified during the policy period or a limited period thereafter). In certain circumstances the court may hold the claims made provision to be void as against Belgium's Loi du 25.6.92 sur le contrat d'assurance terrestre.[83]

Finally, in a consumer transaction the mandatory rules of the law of the country in which the consumer is habitually resident may sometimes apply (art 5). This is discussed in the next section.

It will probably be difficult in any particular case to predict which mandatory rules a court will find to be applicable, let alone how the court will perform the 'extremely delicate task'[84] of combining those rules with the generally applicable law. This difficulty is particularly acute in relation to art 7(1). These provisions, whilst arguably of some benefit to policyholders, do nothing to further the Convention's objectives of dispelling doubt regarding which rules of law apply to any given contract.

In addition to the provisions relating to mandatory rules, article 16 of the Convention permits the court to refuse to apply any rule of the applicable law if its application would be 'manifestly incompatible' with the public policy of the forum. According to the Report[85] this is a 'precise and restrictively worded' exception and may be invoked only where *in the actual case* the relevant provision of the applicable law would lead to consequences which are contrary to the public policy of the forum (including, by implication, the public policy of the EC).[86]

---

83. It is, however, arguable that this rule is not properly classed as mandatory: see n 78, above.
84. Report, at p 28.   85. At p 38.
86. As to the English courts' approach to public policy see Dicey & Morris, *The Conflict of Laws*, 12th edn, pp 1277–84.

## Special rules applying to consumer contracts

Article 5 of the Convention provides that in a contract to supply goods or services (including insurance)[87] to a person ('the consumer'), where no choice of law has been made the law applicable to the contract shall be the law of the consumer's habitual residence.[88] If a choice of law has been made it cannot deprive the consumer of the protection of the mandatory rules of the law of his or her country of habitual residence.[89] The provisions of art 5 apply only if three conditions are satisfied.

First, the goods or services must be supplied for a purpose which can be regarded as outside the consumer's trade or profession.[90] The consumer protection provisions will still apply if the consumer is acting partly within their trade or profession but not 'primarily' so. However, perhaps surprisingly, they will not apply if the supplier reasonably believes that the consumer was acting within their trade or profession when, in fact, the consumer was not.[91]

> Example: A jeweller orders insurance for his or her personal jewellery using their business notepaper; the insurer was not aware that the insurance was effected for purposes outside the insured's trade. Article 5 does not apply.

Secondly, in a contract for services, the provisions will not apply if the services are to be supplied exclusively outside the country of the consumer's habitual residence.[92]

Thirdly, either of the following must have taken place in the country of the consumer's habitual residence:

(a) Before the conclusion of the contract a specific invitation was addressed to the consumer or by advertising, and the consumer took all the necessary steps on his or her part to conclude the contract.[93] The Report states[94] that the invitation must have been aimed specifically at that country. So if a policyholder living in Germany replies to an advertisement in an American publication, even if the publication is sold in Germany, the provisions will probably apply only if the publication was a special edition intended for European countries. The invitation may be made directly, by canvassing or through middlemen:[95] this may be wide enough to cover the

---

87. Report, at p 23.    88. Article 5(3).    89. Article 5(2).    90. Article 5(1).
91. Report, at p 23.    92. Article 5(4)(b).    93. Article 5(2)(a).    94. At pp 23–4.
95. Report, at p 24.

situation where a broker contacts a prospective insured to recommend a policy. In the context of insurance, 'the necessary steps' are likely to include the completion of the proposal form.

(b) The supplier or the supplier's agent received the consumer's order.[96] The word 'agent' covers all persons acting on behalf of the supplier.[97] It covers branch offices[98] and it is possible that it extends to brokers.

# The Second Non-Life Directive

## Outline of the Directive's rules for determining the applicable law

The applicable law rules in the Second Non-Life Directive ('the Directive') apply to contracts of direct insurance covering non-life risks situated in the EC. For some contracts, where protection of the policyholder was considered to be unnecessary, the Directive permits the parties to choose the law of any country to govern their contract. For other contracts, where there was considered to be a need to provide protection to the policyholder, the Directive provides that the parties may make their choice only from a limited number of laws, depending on the circumstances. In either case, if the parties do not make a valid choice of law the court will apply the law of the country (out of those which the parties were entitled to choose) with which the contract is most closely connected: the rebuttable presumption is that the contract is most closely connected with the member state in which the risk is situated. Regardless of which law applies to the contract generally, the court may in certain circumstances apply mandatory rules of a different law. Finally, special rules apply in the case of compulsory risks. These principles are considered in more detail below.

## Contracts in which a free choice of law may be made

The First Non-Life Directive (as amended) contains a classification of non-life risks; certain of these are classed as 'large risks' whilst the remainder are known as 'mass risks'. The present situation is that the parties have complete freedom to choose the applicable

---

96. Article 5(2)(b).    97. Report, at p 24.    98. Ibid at p 24.

law in *any* contract insuring large risks. This situation was effected in stages by three Directives the relevant provisions of which are summarised below.

### The Second Non-Life Directive

The normal jurisdictional rule laid down by this Directive is that the parties have a restricted freedom of choice (see below). However art 7(1)(f) granted freedom of choice in respect of a few large risks, namely classes 4 (railway rolling stock), 5 (aircraft), 6 (ships), 7 (goods in transit), 11 (aircraft liability) and 12 (liability for ships).

### Directive 90/618/EEC [99]

This Directive redefined classes 3 (land vehicles) and 10 (motor vehicle liability) as large risks. This had no effect for the purpose of determining the applicable law until the Third Non-Life Directive was implemented (see below).

### The Third Non-Life Directive [100]

This Directive, by amending the Second Non-Life Directive, extended freedom of choice to contracts insuring *any* large risk. The additional classes thus covered are:

(a) classes 3 (land vehicles) and 10 (motor vehicle liability); [101]
(b) classes 14 (credit) and 15 (suretyship) where the policyholder is engaged professionally in an industrial or commercial activity or in a profession and the risks relate to such activity;
(c) classes 8 (fire and natural forces), 9 (other damage to property), 13 (general liability) and 16 (miscellaneous financial loss) where the policyholder exceeds certain criteria [102] as to size and financial status. [103]

> Example: A large corporation insures a factory in the EC in respect of fire risks. The Second Non-Life Directive, as amended by the

---

[99]. OJ 1990 L330/44. The relevant provision is art 2.
[100]. OJ 1992 L228/1. The relevant provision is art 27.
[101]. Reclassified as a large risk by Directive 90/618/EEC as discussed above.
[102]. As to which see p 10.
[103]. Each member state may add to this list risks insured by professional associations, joint ventures or temporary groupings.

Third Non-Life Directive, would permit the parties to choose any law (e.g., New York law) to govern their contract.

## Circumscribed choice of law

In contracts insuring risks other than those referred to above, the parties have only limited freedom to choose the applicable law. The following rules apply.

### 1. Where the policyholder's habitual residence or central administration is in the member state in which the risk is situated (art 7(1)(a))

Where a policyholder has their habitual residence (if an individual) or its central administration (if a legal person) in the member state in which the risk is situated, the parties may choose the law of that member state; if the law of that member state so allows, the parties may choose the law of another country.

The extent to which the member states' laws grant the parties additional freedom of choice varies widely. Under English law the validity of the parties' choice is tested by applying the rules of the Rome Convention[104] notwithstanding that art 1(3) of the Convention expressly excludes its rules from applying to contracts within the ambit of the Second Non-Life Directive; thus the parties have complete freedom of choice. A similar approach is taken by Dutch law.[105] A free choice of law is permitted by Italian law, subject expressly to mandatory rules of Italian law.[106] However, Belgian law[107] and Spanish law[108] do not permit the parties to choose another law in such cases. German law[109] permits the parties to choose a different law only where the policyholder, being habitually resident in Germany, takes out insurance with an insurer which does not conduct any insurance business in Germany either itself or through intermediaries.

Example: A policyholder who is habitually resident in England insures their house in London. The contract will be governed by

---

104. Insurance Companies Act 1982, Sched 3A, Pt 1, para 5(2)(a).
105. *Wet Conflictenrecht Schadeverzekering* of 18.4.91, art 5(a).
106. Legislative Decree No 175 of 17.3.95, art 122(2).
107. *Loi relative au contrôle des entreprises d'assurances du 9.7.75*, art 28ter.
108. *Ley 30/1995 de 8 de noviembre de Ordenación y Supervisión de los Seguros Privados*, art 107(2).
109. *Einführungsgesetz zu dem Gesetz über den Versicherungsvertrag*, s 9.

English law. However, if the parties have chosen a different law to govern the contract then (as English law would permit such a choice) their choice will be upheld.

It is necessary to bear in mind that (apart from buildings, motor vehicles, travel and holiday risks) risks are considered[110] to be situated in the member state where the policyholder has their habitual residence (if an individual) or its 'establishment, to which the contract relates' (if a legal person). Therefore, if the policyholder is an individual then (subject to the above exceptions and assuming that he or she is habitually resident within the EC) the policyholder will inevitably have their habitual residence in the member state in which the risk is considered situated and the contract will be governed by their home law (or a law which their home law permits to be chosen).

### 2. Where the policyholder's habitual residence or central administration is not in the member state in which the risk is situated (art 7(1)(b))

Where the policyholder's habitual residence or central administration is not in the member state where the risk is situated, the parties may choose *either* the law of the country in which the policyholder has his or her habitual residence or central administration *or* the law of the member state in which the risk is situated.

> Example: A policyholder who is habitually resident in New York insures a house in Portugal. The parties would be free to choose Portuguese law or New York law to govern the contract. (Additional choices may also be available as a result of art 7(1)(d) as described at point 4 below.)

For the reason stated above this article is of most relevance where the insured risk comprises buildings, motor vehicles, or travel and holiday risks or where the policyholder's habitual residence or central administration is not in an EC member state.

### 3. Where the policy insures two or more risks situated in different member states which relate to the policyholder's commercial or industrial activity or profession (art 7(1)(c))

Where the policyholder pursues a commercial or industrial activity or a profession and the contract covers two or more risks which

110. Pursuant to art 2(d): see pp 131–2 .

relate to these activities and which are situated in different member states, the parties may, as an alternative to any other choice which may be permitted under art 7(1), choose the law of the country where the policyholder has their habitual residence or central administration or the law of any of the member states in which the risk is situated.

> Example: A company with its central administration in Belgium insures its factories in the Netherlands and Germany. The parties may choose Belgian, Dutch or German law.

### 4. Where the member states referred to in art 7(1)(b) and (c) grant the parties greater freedom to choose the applicable law (art 7(1)(d))[111]

Article 7(1)(d) of the Directive provides that where 'the Member States referred to' in art 7(1)(b) and (c) grant greater freedom of choice the parties may take advantage of this freedom. Thus the parties may have a choice of a wider range of laws than would otherwise be permitted under art 7(1)(b) and (c).

> Example: A policyholder who is habitually resident in New York insures a house in England. The parties would be able to choose English law or New York law under art 7(1)(b). Under art 7(1)(d) they would also be permitted to choose any law which English law permits to be chosen (the parties may not take advantage of any additional freedom of choice which would be available under the law of New York as New York is not an EC member state).

The only 'member states' referred to in art 7(1)(b) and (c) are the member states in which insured risks are situated.[112] It is not clear whether, for art 7(1)(d) to apply, all of these member states' laws must allow the parties such freedom or whether it is sufficient that only one of them does so. To return to the above example of a Belgian company insuring factories in the Netherlands and Germany, if the parties chose New York law to govern their agreement and such a choice was permitted under Dutch law but not under German law, on a liberal interpretation of art 7(1)(d) the choice would be valid but on a restrictive interpretation it would not be. It is arguable that, as the policyholders in question

---

111. As to the freedom of choice permitted by the laws of various member states see the commentary on art 7(1)(a) above.

112. Article 7(1)(b) and (c) use the word 'country' in relation to the state in which the policyholder has their habitual residence or its central administration.

will tend to be relatively sophisticated, the liberal interpretation is to be preferred.

### 5. Where the risks are limited to events occurring in one member state other than the one in which the risk is situated (art 7(1)(e))

Article 7(1)(e) provides that where 'the risks covered by the contract are limited to events occurring in one Member State other than the Member State where the risk is situated, as defined in art 2(d), the parties may always choose the law of the former State'. This rule therefore provides the parties with an additional choice to those discussed above.

> Example: An individual who is habitually resident in England insures a painting in respect of damage occurring to it in France only. By virtue of art 2(d) the painting is considered to be situated in England. Article 7(1)(e) would permit the parties to choose French law. (Additional choices may also be available under the other rules discussed above, notably art 7(1)(a).)

## Applicable law where no valid choice has been made

A choice of law will not be upheld unless it is 'expressed or demonstrated with reasonable certainty by the terms of the contract or the circumstances of the case';[113] in this respect the Directive adopts the same approach as art 3(1) of the Convention.[114] If the parties have not made a choice of law which satisfies this requirement, or they have made a choice which is not permitted by the rules in art 7(1)(a) to (e), then the court will apply the law of the country with which the contract is most closely connected. This law must be selected from those which the parties could validly have chosen under the above rules.[115]

There is a rebuttable presumption that the contract is most closely connected with the member state in which the risk is situated. This will usually be the member state in which the insured is habitually resident or has its establishment to which the contract relates, except where the risk comprises buildings, motor vehicles or travel and holiday risks. This contrasts with the equivalent presumption in the Rome Convention, which determines the applicable law by reference to the insurer's place of business.[116]

---

113. Article 7(h).     114. See pp 138–40.     115. Article 7(1)(h).     116. See pp 140–2.

Example: A policyholder in England insures a house in France with a Belgian insurer; the contract is silent as to the applicable law. There will be a presumption that French law applies.

The Directive gives no indication of the circumstances in which the presumption may be overruled. One circumstance in which it may be appropriate to override the presumption is where the policyholder and insurer are situated in the same country and insure a risk which is situated in a different country (for example, where a policyholder in England enters into a contract with an insurer in England to insure a house in France). The presumption is unlikely to be overruled if the insured's habitual residence or its central administration is in the member state where the risk is situated.

The presumption was considered in the recent English case *Crédit Lyonnais v New Hampshire Insurance Company*.[117] A US insurance group participated in the worldwide insurance programme of a multinational policyholder whose central administration was in France. Under the programme each of the policyholder's foreign branches or subsidiaries had its own policies, issued by US insurers which were members of the group. The terms of the policies were agreed in France between the policyholder, the policyholder's broker and the insurance group (all of whom were in Paris) and were imposed on the local branch or subsidiary: the branch or subsidiary had no autonomy regarding the cover provided. The policyholder's UK branch or subsidiary had the benefit of two policies under the programme. These were broked by an English broker in London and issued by an English underwriting agency. They expressly provided that all premiums were payable through the brokers in London, and all claims were paid in England. The deductibles, limits of cover and premiums were expressed in French currency and one of the policies referred to provisions of the French Penal Code 'or any other similar legal provisions outside France'. Neither policy contained a choice of law or jurisdiction. The policyholder brought a claim under the policies which was within the limitation period under English law but which would have been time barred if the policies were governed by French law. It was common ground that the insured risk was situated in England and thus that the presumption was in favour of English law, but the insurer

---

117. 16 September 1996 (unreported).

153

argued that the presumption should be overridden because the policies were most closely connected with France.

Barbara Dohmann QC, sitting as a Deputy Judge in the Commercial Court, stated that the court had to determine the country with which the two policies, and not the worldwide programme as a whole, were most closely connected. The fact that the precise terms of the local contracts were dictated by the policyholder's head office in another country did not mean that the contracts were governed by the law of the head office. The Deputy Judge drew attention to the fact that the policyholder was unlikely to have been in a weak bargaining position and could have attempted to stipulate French law and jurisdiction in the policies in order to ensure the homogeneity of its scheme worldwide if this had been its intention, but it had not done so: this left the impression that such homogeneity was neither attempted nor achieved. In view of the facts that the policies were issued in England by an English underwriting agency to a UK branch or subsidiary, expressly and exclusively with respect to that UK business, the Deputy Judge concluded that the presumption was not rebutted and the contracts were governed by English law.

## Dépeçage

Like the Rome Convention, the Directive provides[118] that different laws may govern different parts of the same contract. The part to be severed must have a closer connection with another country (which must be one of the countries considered in art 7(1)). Severance may be effected only 'by way of exception'.

## Mandatory rules

Whichever law applies to the contract generally the court may apply mandatory rules of a different law in three circumstances.

First, where all the elements (except the choice of law)[119] relevant to the situation at the time of the choice of law are connected with one member state only, the choice of law 'shall not

---

118. Article 7(1)(h).
119. It would appear that a choice of jurisdiction is an element which must be taken into consideration for the purpose of this article, in contrast to the position under the equivalent provision (art 3(3)) in the Rome Convention. Under art 12 of the Brussels Convention a choice of jurisdiction in relation to an insurance contract will be valid only in certain circumstances (see pp 118–22).

... prejudice' the application of the mandatory rules of the law of that member state (art 7(1)(g)).

> Example: An English employer takes out employers' liability insurance; the contract is expressly governed by the law of member state X but in all other respects the situation is connected only with England; a dispute arises and the parties agree to bring the claim before a court in state X. The court may strike down any terms in the contract which are prohibited under the Employers' Liability (Compulsory Insurance) Act 1969[120] (assuming that such prohibitions are mandatory rules of English law). (In connection with this example, however, it should be noted that special rules may apply to compulsory risks, as described below and in the next section.)

Secondly, where rules of the law of the forum are mandatory irrespective of the law applicable to the contract, the application of such rules is not restricted (art 7(2), first paragraph). Under the Brussels Convention the forum in which an insurance dispute is brought will usually be the policyholder's country of domicile.[121] This provision of the Directive therefore tends to have the effect of ensuring that the mandatory rules of the policyholder's country of domicile remain applicable.

> Example: An individual who is habitually resident in England insures an apartment situated in London with an American insurer under a contract expressly governed by New York law (this choice would be valid under art 7(1)(a) of the Directive); the insurer refuses to pay a claim, relying on a term which would be in contravention of the Unfair Terms in Consumer Contracts Regulations 1994;[122] the dispute is heard by an English court. Section 7 of those Regulations provides that the Regulations 'shall apply notwithstanding any contract term which applies or purports to apply the law of a non member State, if the contract has a close connection with the territory of the member States'. The Regulations are therefore mandatory rules and the court could strike down the offending term.

Thirdly, if 'the law of a Member State so stipulates, the mandatory rules of the law of the Member State in which the risk

---

120. Such terms are identified in the Employers' Liability (Compulsory Insurance) General Regulations 1971, SI 1971 No 1117.
121. See pp 102, 112–13.
122. SI 1994 No 3159.

is situated or of the Member State imposing the obligation to take out insurance may be applied if and in so far as, under the law of those States, those rules must be applied whatever the law applicable to the contract' (art 7(2), second paragraph).

Under this provision the mandatory rules of two member states may be applied, namely (i) the member state in which the risk is situated or (ii) if the insurance is compulsory, the member state which imposes the obligation to take out the insurance. For either of these mandatory rules to apply two conditions must be satisfied. First, the mandatory rules must be mandatory whatever the law applicable to the contract. Secondly, the law of 'a Member State' must stipulate that the mandatory rules may be applied. It may be inferred, from the first paragraph of art 7(2), that 'the law of a Member State' refers to the law of the forum rather than the law of *any* member state. This rule is not conducive to legal certainty and it has not been implemented in English law.

## Special rules applicable to compulsory risks

Article 8 (as amended by art 30 of the Third Non-Life Directive) concerns insurance which is compulsory under member states' national laws. Each member state is required to provide the Commission with details of its compulsory risks,[123] for publication in the Official Journal.[124] The Commission is in the process of compiling a list of the information which it has received from member states and it is hoped that this will be published before the end of 1996.

The obligation to take out insurance is satisfied only if the contract complies with the specific requirements laid down by the member state[125] and affords a degree of protection to third parties in the case of cessation of cover.[126]

Article 8(3) provides that where the law of the member state in which the risk is situated and the law of the member state imposing the obligation to take out the insurance contradict each other, the latter shall prevail.

---

123. Article 8(5)(a).
124. Article 8(5)(b).
125. Article 8(2).
126. Formerly art 8(4)(d), now renumbered art 8(4)(c) by art 30(1) of the Third Non-Life Directive.

Member states may derogate from the rules set out in art 7 of the Directive by laying down that the law applicable to a compulsory insurance contract is the law of the state imposing the obligation to take out insurance (art 8(4)(b)).[127] Most, but not all, of the member states have exercised this option.

> Example: An insured in France obtains cover in respect of a large risk from an English insurer; the risk is of a kind which French law requires to be insured; the contract contains an express choice of English law. French law[128] has exercised the option conferred by art 8(4)(b) whereas English law has not. An English court would find that the contract is governed by English law whilst a French court would find that the contract is governed by French law.

### Provision of information regarding the applicable law

Article 31 of the Third Non-Life Directive introduces a requirement that before an insurance contract is concluded the insurer must give the insured information regarding the applicable law. Where the parties do not have a free choice of law the insurer must inform the policyholder of the law applicable to the contract. Where the parties are permitted a free choice, the insurer must inform the insured of this fact together with the law which the insurer proposes to choose.

## The Second Life Directive

The Second Life Directive's rules on choice of law apply to any contract of direct insurance covering life risks where the policyholder's habitual residence (if an individual) or 'establishment, to which the contract relates' (if a legal person) is in an EC member state (this state is known as 'the member state of the commitment').

The rules for determining the applicable law are set out in art 4. The applicable law is generally that of the member state of the commitment.[129] There are two exceptions to this. First, where that

---

127. Formerly art 8(4)(c), renumbered by art 30(1) of the Third Non-Life Directive.
128. *Code des Assurances*, art L-182-1.
129. Article 4(1).

law permits the parties to choose the law of another country the parties may take advantage of this freedom.[130]

> Example: A Belgian national who is habitually resident in Belgium insures their life with a French insurance company. Belgian law will, *prima facie*, apply. However, if the parties have chosen a different law then their choice will be upheld if it is permitted by Belgian law.

Secondly, where the policyholder is an individual whose habitual residence is in a member state other than that of which he or she is a national, the parties may choose the law of the member state of which he or she is a national.[131]

> Example: A Dutch national who is habitually resident in Belgium insures their life with a French insurance company. Belgian law *prima facie* applies but the parties could instead choose Dutch law. Alternatively, pursuant to the previous exception, the parties could choose any other law which Belgian law permits to be chosen.

Where a state includes several territorial units, each having its own rules of law, each unit is to be considered a country for the purposes of identifying the applicable law.[132]

## Mandatory rules

The mandatory rules of a different law may apply in two circumstances.[133] First, the Directive does not restrict the application of those rules of the forum which are mandatory irrespective of the law applicable to the contract. Secondly, if 'the law of a Member State so stipulates', the mandatory rules of the law of the member state of the commitment may be applied in so far as (under the law of that member state) those rules must be applied whatever the law applicable to the contract. These provisions are similar to those in art 7(2) of the Second Non-Life Directive.[134]

---

130. Article 4(1). Under English law the parties' freedom of choice is to be determined by reference to the rules in the Rome Convention: Insurance Companies Act 1982, Sched 3A, Pt II, para 10(2).
131. Article 4(2).
132. Article 4(3). It is not clear how the courts would determine the part of the United Kingdom of which a person is a national.
133. Article 4(4).
134. See pp 154–6.

# CHAPTER SEVEN

# Insurance and competition law

## Outline of competition policy

### Basic theory

Free competition forms a key policy objective of almost all advanced economies. The reasons for this are straightforward. Economic theory dictates that a monopoly supplier, unlike a supplier facing strong competition, can, by regulating their output, influence the price at which their product will sell to consumers, and the same theory goes on to demonstrate that a monopoly supplier maximises profits by supplying less of the product but at a higher price.[1] A monopolist may also adopt undesirable practices as a result of a monopoly position. First, the monopolist may adopt 'exclusionary' practices aimed at maximising the market share: these may include predatory undercutting of such competitors as may exist, foreclosing distribution outlets by offering uneconomic discounts to distributors, and mass advertising. Secondly, the monopolist may drift into 'productive inefficiency' in that, as a result of not facing competition, quality of product and service may diminish and investment may tail off, all through lack of incentive to improve. It is worthy of note that these problems are not inevitable, but are merely dangers which flow from the existence of a monopoly position.[2]

1. The consequence of this is 'allocative inefficiency', i.e., that some consumers are unable to afford to purchase their first choice product, and thus have to choose some other product, and this in turn leads to resources being used to produce more of that product to meet demand. Resources are thereby misallocated.

2. Thus, in the UK, there is no prohibition as such on monopoly. However, the practices of monopolists in so far as they are thought to offend the public interest, may be investigated by the Director General of Fair Trading under the Competition Act 1980 (the 'anti-competitive practice' procedure) or, in the

Monopoly supply is one problem: agreements between competitors is another. Some types of agreement between competitors are clearly highly desirable: little objection can generally be taken to agreements which reduce costs, e.g., by shared marketing and distribution arrangements, or agreements which lead to new products coming onto the market by shared risk-bearing, e.g., research and development agreements. Other types of agreement are, however, almost inevitably harmful. Where suppliers come together and fix the prices of their products and impose restrictions on output (e.g., by dividing the market on a geographical, customer or quota basis), and given that the agreed prices will have to be fixed at a level which keeps the most inefficient supplier profitable, the most efficient suppliers are necessarily prevented from expanding their output and offering lower prices to customers. The dangers of monopoly are, by means of such restrictive agreements, simulated.

The final major problem is that of mergers. If competitors merge to form a larger enterprise, monopoly may result and at the very least the consequence will be the equivalent of a price and output agreement. Equally, if the merger is vertical, i.e., takes place between suppliers and distributors rather than competitors, there is a possible danger that competing suppliers may lose access to distribution channels previously open to them.[3]

The economic reasons, based on consumer protection, for the maintenance of competition are, therefore, compelling, and partially explain the adoption of competition rules in the Treaty of Rome.[4] However, an equally important factor in EC law, and one which is necessarily not relevant to pure domestic regulation, is the additional problems which anti-competitive conduct can pose for the concept of a single market. A monopolist may take advantage of variations between national preferences by adopting a differential pricing scheme in each member state, enforceable only by imposing strict territorial limits upon chosen distributors: such

---

2. *(continued)* context of a more general inquiry into the industry as a whole, by the Monopolies and Mergers Commission under the Fair Trading Act 1973 (the monopoly reference procedure).

3. Mergers are regulated in the UK under the Fair Trading Act 1973, under which a reference may be made to the Monopolies and Mergers Commission by a government minister in those cases in which a satisfactory resolution cannot be reached by prior negotiations conducted by the Director General of Fair Trading.

4. And, indeed, in the Coal and Steel Treaty, arts 65 and 66.

limits will typically take the form of an export ban, whereby each distributor is allocated a particular territory and is forbidden to solicit or to meet orders from potential customers outside that territory. Equally, even in the absence of monopoly, a distributor may be unwilling to bear the costs and risks of promoting and selling goods within their territory in the absence of some form of promise by the original supplier that the distributor will receive exclusivity and will not face competition from imports. The imposition of exclusivity in distribution, by so-called 'vertical restraints', whether demanded by the supplier or distributors or by all of the parties, gives rise to an irreconcilable conflict with the basic concept of the EC, which is to allow goods and services to cross national barriers without restriction. Consequently, much of the focus of EC competition is directed at distribution arrangements in a manner which is not always reflected in purely domestic legislation.[5]

## The competition rules of the EC [6]

### Administration

EC competition law is concerned with three matters: agreements which prevent, restrict or distort competition in a manner which affects trade between member states (art 85 of the Treaty of Rome); abuse of dominant position within the EC (art 86), and concentrations with a Community dimension which are not compatible with the Community (Council Regulation 4064/89 on the control of concentrations between undertakings, generally referred to as the Merger Regulation).

The regulatory authority for each of these aspects of policy is the European Commission, which has, under powers delegated to it by the Council of Ministers under Council Regulation 1 7/6, the function of investigating potential infringements and bringing

5. In the UK, for example, the Restrictive Trade Practices Act 1976 imposes a prima facie ban upon 'horizontal' agreements between competitors, but the Act excludes pure 'vertical' distribution agreements. The latter are capable of challenge only following an administrative investigation by the Director General of Fair Trading under the Competition Act 1980 or by the Monopolies and Mergers Commission under the Fair Trading Act 1973.

6. Identical rules apply as between EC and EFTA countries under the EEA Agreement, although where EFTA is concerned the relevant enforcement authority is the Supervisory Authority established under the EEA Agreement. In June 1996 the UK published the draft of a Competition Bill that would bring UK law on restrictive agreements into line with EC law.

established infringements to an end. Appeals from Commission decisions on point of fact or law may be brought before the Court of First Instance, and a further appeal on point of law only lies to the European Court of Justice. In some instances domestic competition authorities may possess jurisdiction over matters falling also within the competence of the Commission, although this is comparatively rare as the Commission is concerned with cross-border issues whereas domestic authorities primarily regulate their national markets: where such a conflict does arise, and the domestic authority does decide to press ahead with its own proceedings despite the Commission's interest, the Commission's final decision must prevail in the event of a conflict.[7]

In this way, competition policy is primarily enforced by administrative proceedings. However, it was established at an early stage in the development of the law that arts 85 and 86 are both directly effective, in that they can be relied upon as between private parties in domestic litigation.[8] An infringement of EC competition law may, therefore, give rise to a private cause of action resulting in damages or injunctive relief,[9] or it may operate as a defence to proceedings in which it is, for example, asserted that the defendant is in breach of a supply contract and in which the defendant asserts that the contract is void under EC law.[10] Reference, under art 177 of the Treaty of Rome, may be made to the European Court of Justice by domestic courts faced with arguments based on the meaning of arts 85 and 86, and in this way much of the case law on the interpretation and application of these articles has been determined by the ECJ by means of preliminary rulings. In some situations a domestic court may be faced with an issue which has been or is being considered by the Commission: here, the relationship between the two institutions is governed by a Commission Notice issued in 1993.[11]

7. As decided in Case 253/78 *Procureur de la République v Giry and Guerlain* [1981] 2 CMLR 99. It remains uncertain whether all forms of clearance by the Commission preclude domestic condemnation. The Commission issued a draft notice dealing with these matters in October 1996.
8. Case 127/73 *Belgische Radio en Televisie v SABAM* [1974] 2CMLR 238.
9. As far as the UK is concerned, see *Garden Cottage Foods v Milk Marketing Board* [1984] AC 130.
10. As regards the UK, the relevant principles were most recently discussed by the Court of Appeal in *Chiron Corporation v Murex Diagnostics Ltd (No 2)* [1994] 1 CMLR 410.
11. Commission Notice on co-operation between national courts and the Commission in applying arts 85 and 86 of the Treaty of Rome, OJ 1993 C39/6. In outline, the court must follow a decision reached by the Commission.

*Restrictive agreements*

Article 85(1) of the Treaty of Rome outlaws agreements between undertakings, decisions of associations of undertakings and concerted practices which affect trade between member states and which have the object or effect of preventing, restricting or distorting competition within the common market. Any infringing agreement is void by virtue of art 85(2). Article 85(1) catches everything from bilateral agreements to recommendations of trade associations, even if such recommendations are not followed by all members of the association.[12] The agreement must, however, be capable of having some impact in more than one member state, and the agreement must either be intended to restrict competition or must have the effect of doing so given the structure of the market in which it operates.[13] Agreements which have a *de minimis* effect on competition are outside art 85(1), and this is presumed to be the case where the turnover of the parties does not exceed 300 million ecu.[14]

Where the Commission becomes aware of a potentially unlawful agreement, it has wide powers to undertake an investigation and to obtain information from the parties: non-compliance with the Commission's inquiries can result in heavy fines.[15] In practice, the majority of agreements which might potentially be caught by art 85(1) are notified to the Commission under the procedure set out in Commission Regulation 3385/94. Notification is not mandatory, but has two major advantages from the parties' point of view: only notified agreements can be exempted from art 85(1) by the Commission under its powers in art 85(3): and once an agreement has been notified the parties cannot be fined for subsequent conduct in operating the agreement. Following its investigation the Commission may reach a formal decision that the agreement is outside art 85(1) ('negative clearance'), that it infringes art 85(1) or, in the case of a notified

---

11. *(continued)* However, it is unclear whether the court can give effect to a 'comfort letter' issued by the Commission terminating art 85 proceedings, as such a letter does not amount to an exemption; only the Commission can grant exemption.
12. Cases T39-40/92 *Groupement des Cartes Bancaires 'CB' and Eurocheque International v Commission* [1994] II-ECR 49.
13. See Case C-234/89 *Delimitis v Henninger Bräu AG* [1991] ECR I-935, [1992] 5 CMLR 210.
14. Commission Notice on agreements of minor importance 1986, OJ 1986 C231/2.
15. The Commission's investigatory powers, and the rules on proceedings before the Commission are set out in Commission Regulation 99/63.

agreement only, that it infringes art 85(1) but should be exempted under art 85(3). In practice, formal decisions are the exception rather than the rule, and the matter is commonly dealt with by means of a 'comfort letter' to the parties terminating the inquiry.

Article 85(1) itself provides a non-exhaustive list of agreements which may be taken to infringe its terms, and in addition the Commission has developed its own substantial jurisprudence on the ambit of art 85. Article 85(3) permits exemption in the case of agreements which contribute to economic progress, which allow consumers a fair share of the benefits, which go no further than necessary to achieve their aim and which do not eliminate competition – these elements are cumulative and not alternative.

In outline, the application of art 85 has been as follows. Article 85(1) is infringed by any agreement which fixes prices and output and delimits geographical markets. Exemption under art 85(3) is almost certain not to be available in these cases. By contrast, distribution agreements, and horizontal restraints which are intended to reduce costs and stimulate research will benefit from art 85(3) exemption. Given the sheer volume of agreements which fall within the Commission's jurisdiction, the Commission has over the years made increasing use of its power[16] to grant block exemption to entire classes of agreement, based upon its experience of dealing with many individual notifications. A large number of block exemptions presently exist, dealing with matters such as exclusive dealing and purchasing, technology transfer agreements (patent and know-how licensing), franchising, research and development, and transport. As will be seen later in this chapter, insurance has benefited from a specific block exemption. The block exemptions follow a more or less consistent pattern, listing contract terms which are regarded by the Commission as harmless to competition, terms which do restrict competition but which, subject to conditions, may be included in an agreement, and terms which, if included, automatically deprive the agreement of the benefit of the block exemption: the final group of so-called 'black list' terms is concerned particularly with unjustified market division. Where a block exemption exists, an agreement falling within its terms need not be notified to the Commission.

---

16. Technically, the power stems from the Council, which adopts a Council Regulation authorising the Commission to issue a block exemption in the form of a Commission Regulation: the Council does, however, act in accordance with the Commission's own recommendations as to when an enabling Council Regulation should be issued.

*Abuse of dominant position*

Article 86 of the Treaty of Rome outlaws the abuse of a dominant position by one or more undertakings. The abuse must affect trade between member states, and it must affect a substantial part of the EC, although these conditions are normally easily satisfied except in the case of a narrow monopoly located entirely within one member state. Dominance is established by a detailed market analysis undertaken by the Commission, which involves consideration of: (i) the product in question, and in particular whether acceptable substitutes are available; (ii) the geographical area in which the dominance exists; and (iii) whether the dominance is temporary and based on seasonal or other fluctuating factors, or whether it is permanent. The Commission's conclusions on these points are reviewable on appeal, and the European Court of Justice has been wary of findings of dominance based on a very narrow view of the relevant market.[17] Once the market has been delimited, the Commission must determine whether there is dominance within that market, a question which depends partly upon market share – 40% having proved in practice to be significant – and partly upon other factors, including barriers to market entry (i.e., the ease with which competitors may join the market), the nature of actual and potential competition and the countervailing power of persons dealing with the undertaking under investigation.

Where there is a finding of dominance, various forms of potentially abusive conduct are listed by art 86 itself. These include unfair pricing practices, discrimination, and the imposition of unfair terms, including terms requiring purchasers to obtain unrelated goods or services as a condition of supply. There have been comparatively few decisions reached under art 86, and these have tended to concentrate on exclusionary conduct, such as predatory pricing and interfering with supplies to competitors: there has been no firm move towards controlling price levels operated by dominant firms.

---

[17.] Perhaps the most important authority is Case *6/72 Europemballage and Continental Can v European Commission* [1973] ECR 215.

*Mergers*

Prior to the adoption of the Merger Regulation the EC's control over mergers was minimal, and was based on strained applications of arts 85 and 86.[18] Policy was formalised by the adoption of the Regulation, which applies to concentrations[19] between undertakings[20] where there is a 'Community dimension': this term catches mergers where the combined aggregate worldwide turnover[21] of the parties exceeds 5,000 million ecu and the combined EC turnover of the parties exceeds 250 million ecu. Also, to avoid the Regulation encroaching on primarily domestic matters, it will not apply if two-thirds of each of the parties' EC turnover is achieved in the same member state. A joint venture which does not result in permanent structural changes (a 'co-operative joint venture') is outside the Merger Regulation and instead is regulated by art 85(1); by contrast, where the joint venture results in long-term changes (a 'concentrative joint venture') the Merger Regulation applies to it.[22]

Where a merger is within the Regulation, it must be notified to the Commission.[23] The Commission must then decide within strict time limits whether to clear the merger or to undertake an investigation into its compatibility with the common market. In an investigation into compatibility, the Commission is required to consider whether the merger creates or strengthens a dominant position as a result of which competition would be significantly impeded in the EC or a substantial part of the EC.

18. See in particular Cases 142 and 156/84 *BAT and Reynolds v European Commission* [1987] ECR 4487.
19. For the meaning of 'concentration', see the Commission's Notice on the notion of a concentration 1994, OJ 1994 C385/5.
20. For the concept of an 'undertaking', see the Commission's Notice on the notion of undertakings 1994, OJ 1994 C385/12.
21. The concept of turnover is complex, and has been clarified by the Commission's Notice on calculation of turnover 1994, OJ 1994 C385/21. Under proposals published by the Commission in November 1996, the turnover figures in the text would be reduced in all cases, and reduced still further where the merger fell within the domestic rules of at least three member states.
22. The distinction between the two types of joint venture is complex, and has caused the Commission to issue guidelines on at least two separate occasions. The current version of the guidelines is in the Notice on the distinction between concentrative and co-operative joint ventures 1994, OJ 1994 C385/1.
23. The procedures are laid down in Commission Regulation 3384/94.

# Competition in the insurance market

## Insurance and the competition rules

### Applicability of the competition rules

Articles 85 and 86 of the Treaty of Rome refer only to the supply of goods, and it was at one time arguable that services, including financial services such as insurance and banking, fell outside their ambit. The argument was given force by art 87 of the Treaty, which specifically conferred upon the Council of Ministers the power to adopt regulations or directives giving effect to the principles in arts 85 and 86, including by defining the various branches of the economy to which they applied. The financial services sector accordingly argued that, in the absence of any secondary legislation, it was immune from the competition rules, and justified its view by reference to the fact that the financial services sector, particularly banking and insurance, was subject to stringent domestic regulation which was of itself sufficient protection. This approach was denied by the Commission as early as 1973,[24] by stating that 'insurance companies must respect the competition rules in the same way as other undertakings', and the succeeding decade saw the Commission applying the competition rules to a variety of service sectors including broadcasting and banking. Finally, in *Zuchner v Bayerische Vereinsbank AG*[25] in 1980, the ECJ confirmed that Art 85(1) extended to banking services, and in *Verband der Sachversicherer eV v European Commission*[26] in 1987 the position of insurance was put beyond all doubt. The Commission had indeed anticipated the *Zuchner* view of competition and services by objecting to (and without the need for a decision achieving the abandonment of) an arrangement between hull insurers fixing premiums to be charged where cover was transferred as between two participating insurers.[27]

### Impact of the competition rules

As will be seen below, the Commission formalised its approach to agreements between insurers in its block exemption issued in

---

24. Second Report on Competition Policy, point 60.
25. Case 172/80 [1981] ECR 2021.   26. Case 45/85 [1987] ECR 405.
27. EC Bull No 5, 1969. These proceedings are referred to in Maitland-Walker, *EC Insurance Directives* (Lloyd's of London Press, 1992), para 6.5.

1991. In the period leading up to this Regulation, a number of important insurance cases were investigated by the Commission – *Fire Insurance*,[28] *Nuovo CEGAM*,[29] *German Fire Insurance*,[30] *P & I Clubs*,[31] *TEKO*,[32] *Concordato Incendio*[33] and *Assurpol*[34] – and the principles contained in the block exemption were derived from these cases. The *German Fire Insurance* decision was appealed to the ECJ in the *Verband der Sachversicherer eV* case, the Commission's approach there being affirmed. A number of general themes emerged from these cases, and these are consistent with the overall administration of competition policy by the Commission but in the insurance context.

*Rate-fixing* Attempts by insurers to fix net premiums, irrespective of motive, have on principle been condemned. Perhaps the most important decision is that of the ECJ in *Verband der Sachversicherer eV*, where an association of German insurers constituting almost the entire German property insurance market recommended a premium increase for fire and consequential loss cover to its membership: the recommendation was intended to re-establish the viability of the market, but nevertheless was not followed by all of the members. The ECJ, upholding the Commission's decision, ruled that the recommendation amounted to a decision of an association of undertakings, and that it infringed art 85(1) and did not qualify for art 85(3) exemption because its main effect was to eliminate price competition between insurers of differing efficiencies. Moreover, it was unnecessary for the parties to seek to ensure the solvency of all insurers by means of this agreement, as solvency was the concern of the regulatory structure imposed upon insurers by the EC Directives on insurance. One particular feature of this case is the argument by the association that the agreement did not affect trade between member states, as required by art 85(1), as it applied purely to the German market: this contention was rejected, as German branches of foreign insurers were members of the association, this being sufficient to give the agreement an international aspect despite the fact that the German branches were, as a matter of German law, fully autonomous undertakings.

28. OJ 1982 L80/60.   29. [1984] 2 CMLR 484.   30. [1985] 3 CMLR 246.
31. [1989] 4 CMLR 178.   32. [1990] 4 CMLR 957.   33. [1991] 4 CMLR 199.
34. [1993] 4 CMLR 338.

In *Nuovo CEGAM* the agreement, between insurers from Italy and a number of other countries, was intended to generate demand in the engineering industry for insurance against mechanical breakdown. One of its features, common premiums as determined by the association formed by the parties, was held by the Commission to contravene art 85(1). The Commission nevertheless saw no objection to the parties agreeing the level of that part of the premium which related to the risk itself, as this was in effect a joint decision as to the nature of the risk itself based upon shared experience, and was not anti-competitive as the overall level of the premium – taking into account overheads, brokerage and profit – charged by each insurer had not of itself been predetermined: art 85(3) exemption was granted here. In *Assurpol*, exemption was granted to a rate-fixing agreement, subject to its modification to comply with similar criteria.

In *Concordato Incendio* the machinery was less formal, and consisted of recommended premium rates for particular risks which members could accept or reject: this was held to infringe art 85(1), but qualified for art 85(3) exemption on the basis that the parties were free to determine final premium rates for themselves. Similarly, in *P & I Clubs*, which is discussed in more detail below, the Commission struck down an agreement which operated to impose a minimum premium for oil tanker risks, but granted art 85(3) exemption to a modified agreement under which premium levels were required to make sufficient provision for the administration and other costs borne by the insurers.

Agreements to reduce costs have been looked upon more favourably. In *Insurance Intermediaries*[35] the Commission issued a notice indicating that it intended to make a 'favourable decision' regarding an agreement fixing the maximum commission payable by Irish non-life insurers to various categories of intermediary.[36] There is always a danger in fixing maxima that the figure agreed becomes the norm, and it is clear that had the agreement in practice operated in that way it would not have qualified for clearance.

**Standard terms of cover** The delimitation of standard cover by insurers is almost inevitably to be found where there is a

---

35. OJ 1987 C 120/5.
36. No formal decision was ever reached in this case, and it was thus not made clear whether the agreement would have benefited from negative clearance under art 85(1) or exemption under art 85(3).

premium-fixing agreement, as without this, premium-fixing is largely meaningless. Consequently, where the fixing of terms is found to be part of an overall anti-competitive structure, it has been condemned by the Commission: this was the conclusion in *Nuovo CEGAM*, in relation to an agreement to limit the duration of policies offered to policyholding engineering enterprises. *Concordato Incendio* also involved recommended contract terms, and while the recommendation was held to contravene art 85(1) it was nevertheless granted art 85(3) exemption as members were free to depart from it and in practice there was competition between the participants.

*Information exchanges* It has long been appreciated by both national and EC competition authorities that the effects of a formal price-fixing agreement can be replicated by regular information exchanges between competitors, as such exchanges are frequently characterised by an underlying assumption that any (upward) move on prices by one competitor will be followed by others, particularly where they take place under the auspices of a trade association consisting of the leading suppliers. Where information exchanges have been found to have this effect, they have been treated by the Commission as infringing art 85(1). This approach first appeared in *Fire Insurance*,[37] in which the Commission took the view that a trade association recommen- dation as to premium rates for fire insurance amounted to a decision of an association of undertakings contrary to art 85(1), even though the recommendation was not adopted by all members. The reasoning was the same in *Concordato Incendio*. The impact of information exchanges is also demonstrated by *TEKO*, which concerned an association of engineering machinery insurers, established to operate as an information service covering matters such as the assessment of risks and the determination of premiums. Members were not bound by its conclusions, but in practice advice was accepted with the result that premiums and terms were co-ordinated. The Commission was on the facts pre- pared to grant art 85(3) exemption, on the basis that the sharing of costs in risk determination as between the insurers made possible work which would have been difficult to conduct on an individual basis and which also reduced the insurers' aggregate costs for the benefit of assureds.

37. See n 28 above.

It follows from *TEKO* that not all information exchanges are necessarily harmful, and in particular the exchange of information which is relevant to risk-assessment is almost certainly beneficial: the costs of obtaining such information by each individual insurer are reduced, and each insurer is better equipped to make informed underwriting decisions. The *Concordato Incendio* decision is also important in this context, as there the Commission granted art 85(3) exemption to an overall arrangement between Italian fire insurers which, in addition to recommending premium levels for particular risks, included also the collation and distribution of statistical information on fire risks, information on studies on measures to reduce risk and information on opportunities in foreign markets. A similar result was reached in *Assurpol* as regards information exchanges and pooling in the environmental risks market, as the insurers would not individually have been able to take the necessary exercise. As will be seen, these decisions had a significant impact on the subsequent block exemption.

*Restrictions on contracting parties* Insurers deal with many other contracting parties in the course of their business: reinsurance must be placed; in the case of large risks, co-insurers must be found; reputable brokers from whom insurers will receive business channelled from assureds must be identified; and the assureds with whom the insurer is prepared to deal must be known. Agreements between insurers as to the parties with whom they will deal are unlikely to survive a challenge under art 85(1).[38] In *P & I Clubs* the Commission considered the International Group Agreement (IGA) reached between the major marine protection and indemnity clubs: the clubs are in effect associations of shipowners, whose role is to offer marine cover on a mutual and non-profit making basis to their members.[39] The IGA prevented a member of one club

---

38. See also *Re Institute of Independent Insurance Brokers*, [1991] ICR 822, in which the UK's Restrictive Practices Court struck down, under the Restrictive Trade Practices Act 1976, an agreement between insurance brokers to boycott insurers who had entered into an arrangement providing free insurance to purchasers of new Ford cars.

39. Clubs do not refer to themselves as insurers as such, but rather have members who pay contributions to the mutual fund, and it is the fund which pays losses suffered by individual members. Unlike pure insurance premiums, membership contributions are not fixed finally, and may be supplemented by calls on members where there have been substantial losses. P & I clubs specialise in hull and liability insurance.

from transferring to another at a lower membership rate other than on proof that the rate presently being paid was excessive, and any member who wished to leave a club was required to pay a sum to it to cover losses anticipated but not yet crystallised and arising during the period of membership. The clubs persuaded the Commission that the objective of the rules was not anti-competitive, but rather was to secure continuity of membership and of income levels. The Commission accepted the justification, and granted art 85(3) exemption by modifying the rules on the basis that a member should be allowed to transfer unless the rate being offered by the transferee club was unreasonably low, and that liability for future losses was not to be met by a leaving payment but rather by the provision of a bank guarantee.

In *Nuovo CEGAM* the Commission was faced with two relevant terms: (i) co-insurers had to be sought from within the association formed by a group of engineering insurers; and (ii) members of the association were restricted in their choice of reinsurers, the reinsurers being members of the association and obliged to offer reinsurance to members of the association on no less favourable terms than it was offered to insurers outside the association. Both terms were held to contravene art 85(1), but art 85(3) exemption was granted to term (ii), on the basis that it facilitated the obtaining of reinsurance at favourable rates and also encouraged the granting of insurance in the first place, as the availability of reinsurance is a key consideration in the decision whether or not to offer insurance in the first place. This reasoning was echoed in *TEKO*, where the Commission granted art 85(3) exemption to a pool of insurers who agreed that reinsurance would be available only from their own number. However, in *TEKO* the Commission additionally granted exemption under art 85(3) for an agreement between certain of the members only to insure space risks on a co-insurance basis with other members of the association: while this was contrary to art 85(1), exemption was justified by the facts that the type of insurance in question was relatively new and high-risk and that the parties were seeking to establish themselves in the market for such risks so that collaboration increased rather than reduced competition.

There are necessarily other limits to the application of art 85 in this context, and in particular there can be no objection on competition grounds to the exchange of information as to the experience of individual insurers with reinsurers, co-insurers, brokers and policyholders provided that there is no wider anti-competitive context in which this takes place, as again such exchange permits insurers to make informed choices of their own.

## The block exemption

### Scope of the block exemption

In May 1991 the Council of Ministers adopted Council Regulation 1534/91,[40] authorising the Commission to adopt a block exemption for certain classes of insurance agreement. The Regulation listed six forms of co-operation which might be permitted by a block exemption:

(a) the establishment of common risk premium tariffs based on collectively ascertained statistics or the number of claims;
(b) the establishment of common policy conditions;
(c) the common coverage of certain types of risks;
(d) the settlement of claims;
(e) the testing and acceptance of security devices;
(f) registers of, and information on, aggravated risks, provided that the keeping of these registers and the handling of this information is carried out subject to the proper protection of confidentiality.

The block exemption itself, Commission Regulation 2932/92,[41] proved not to be quite as bold. Article 1 of the Regulation extends, in identical words, only to items (a), (b), (c) and (e) of the list in Council Regulation 1534/91: the Commission took the view that it did not have sufficient experience of the operation of common claims settlements and registers on aggravated risks to grant block exemption, and preferred to deal with agreements on these points on a case-by-case basis.

There are in addition other forms of agreement which have come before the Commission under art 85(1) but which fall outside the enabling Council Regulation. Perhaps the most

40. On the application of art 85(3) of the Treaty to certain categories of agreements, decisions and concerted practices in the insurance sector.
41. On the application of art 85(3) of the Treaty to certain categories of agreements, decisions and concerted practices in the insurance sector.

important of these, at least in terms of English practice, is the 'appointed representative' agreement which is found in the life insurance market. Under the Financial Services Act 1986, which applies to most forms of life insurance, an insurer wishing to sell through intermediaries must, under the concept of 'polarisation' use either exclusive ('tied') agents or wholly independent agents. Tied agents are referred to by the 1986 Act as 'appointed representatives', and s 47 of the Act imposes liability upon the insurer for its appointed representatives' errors and omissions. In *Halifax Building Society/Standard Life Assurance Co*[42] an agreement whereby one of the UK's leading building societies agreed to act as the appointed representative of one of the UK's leading life offices was, after negotiation with the Commission, modified in order to delete terms under which the insurer was required to obtain the building society's consent for the appointment of other agents and under which the building society could not pass on its commission to customers. The European Commission was primarily influenced by the market shares of the two parties in their respective markets and the fact that the insurer had obtained exclusivity for its products.

### Structure of the block exemption

The Insurance block exemption follows more or less the pattern established for the numerous other block exemptions adopted by the Commission. The forms of agreement permissible are identified, the terms which they may include are specified (the 'White List') and terms which, if included, remove the benefit of the block exemption (the 'Black List') are included. An agreement which qualifies under the block exemption need not be notified, whereas one which does not qualify, either because it falls outside the listed agreements or because it contains blacklisted terms, must be notified in order for individual exemption to be obtained. Moreover, art 17 contains the familiar provision removing automatic exemption from agreements which, while qualifying under the block exemption, have effects incompatible with the criteria for exemption laid down in art 85(3) of the Treaty of Rome.

42. OJ 1992 C1 31/2.

*Agreements permitted by the block exemption*

*Premium calculation agreements* Article 2 confines the block exemption to two specific types of agreement: (a) the calculation of the average cost of risk cover based on mortality and statistical tables, yielding figures for the chosen period on the number of claims, the number of risks insured and the sums payable by insurers; (b) the carrying out of studies on the impact of external events (e.g., major catastrophes). Article 4 makes it clear that any figures derived from such calculations and studies must not form the basis of an agreement between insurers to use them in premium calculation, and art 3, confirming the case law, requires figures to be produced net of insurers' own administrative and other costs. Article 3 further provides that the figures must not enable individual participating insurers to be identified (in order to prevent any form of price leadership) and must make it clear that the figures are purely illustrative. If the hypotheses on which the figures are based are unjustifiable, the Commission has reserved the power to withdraw the benefit of the block exemption from the agreement under art 17.

*Standard policy conditions* Article 5(1) of the block exemption authorises agreements which have as their object the establishment and distribution of standard policy terms. Reinsurance agreements are excluded, presumably on the basis of the Commission's lack of experience of this market. Article 6 lays down the conditions on which the exemption is based. The effect of this article is that the policy conditions which are developed must be purely illustrative and are not to bind any insurer to adopt them, and must be readily accessible to any interested person.

Moreover, there are certain forms of policy condition, specified in art 7, which may not be included in the agreed standard conditions, apparently on the basis that the terms in question are potentially unfair and that the uniform adoption of them would remove the possibility of individual negotiation. The use of any of these 'Black List' conditions, which have as their most important underlying themes the tying of the assured to a particular insurer or the unavailability of superior coverage in the market, automatically removes the benefit of the block exemption, and exemption is then available only on the basis of individual application. The conditions in the Black List are those which:

(a) exclude risks commonly covered, without indicating specifically that each insurer is free to provide such cover;

(b) impose conditions on certain risks, without indicating specifically that each insurer remains free to waive them;

(c) propose comprehensive cover, including risks in respect of which a significant number of assureds would not normally seek cover, without indicating specifically that each insurer may offer separate cover;

(d) indicate the amount of the excess to be borne by assureds;

(e) allow the insurer to increase the premium or to alter policy coverage without the assured's consent;

(f) allow the insurer to alter policy terms without the assured's consent;

(g) outside life insurance, impose a contract of more than three years' duration on the assured;[43]

(h) impose a renewal period of more than one year on automatic renewal;

(i) require the assured to agree to the reinstatement of a policy which has lapsed owing to the risk having lapsed, where the risk reappears;

(j) require the assured to seek other insurance from the same insurer;

(k) bind an assured who sells the insured subject matter to a third party to transfer the policy as well as the property to the third party.

In addition to these specific prohibited conditions, art 8 of the block exemption removes its benefits from agreements to remove cover from certain categories of risk based on the characteristics of the assured, other than social or occupational characteristics: it is unclear what is intended here, but presumably race and sex issues fall within the prohibition. Finally, as a general sweeping-up provision, the benefit of the block exemption may be removed from an agreement by the Commission under art 17 of the block exemption as regards non-blacklisted terms, where such terms

---

43. Life policies are necessarily continuous for the period of years specified in them, whereas non-life policies are periodic and on renewal a fresh contract is created. A non-life policy of lengthy duration is regarded as tying the assured to the insurer, and cannot be imposed. However, lengthy non-life policies are regularly used in some contexts, e.g., for long-term construction projects. The key word here is *imposed*.

create 'to the detriment of the policyholder, a significant imbalance between the rights and obligations arising from the contract'.[44]

Article 5(2) extends the block exemption to the creation of models illustrating the profits to be made from life policies, but art 9 removes the exemption where the models go further and identify specific interest rates and include an element for overheads and costs, as such inclusions render collective rate-fixing relatively easy. The exemption will also be lost if the parties agree to adhere only to the illustrative models.

*Common coverage of certain types of risk*  Article 10 permits insurers and reinsurers to participate in co-insurance/reinsurance pools. It is not concerned with *ad hoc* agreements between insurers to insure specific risks on a co-insurance basis. The arrangements which are contemplated here are rather longer term and are common in practice. Typically, a group of insurers or reinsurers will be formed to accept risks of a given description in agreed proportions: the group, generally referred to as a pool, will normally be managed by an underwriting agent who is given authority by the pool members to accept risks on their behalf. Article 10 allows the participants to reach agreement on matters such as the nature of the risks to be covered, the conditions of membership and withdrawal, proportions of liability which each member will accept, and how the pool is to be managed. Article 12 (echoed by art 13 for reinsurance) further permits the pool agreement to make provision for common premiums and cover, common claims settlement and an obligation on each member not to reinsure their share of the risk but to bear it for their own account.

In order to prevent competition being unduly restricted, art 11 imposes market share limits upon the participants. The parties to an agreement must not represent more than 10 per cent (15 per cent in the case of reinsurance) of insurance for the risks and cover provided, and each party must be able to withdraw from the pool subject to a notice period of not more than six months.[45] The market share figures are modified in the case of major risks – catastrophe cover and aggravated risks – for which cover other than by way of co-insurance may be difficult if not impossible to obtain: here, the pool itself may account for only 10 per cent (insurance)

---

44. This wording is identical to that appearing in the Unfair Contract Terms Directive 1991, discussed in chapter 2.
45. Withdrawal can relate only to the acceptance of future risks: the liability of a withdrawing member under existing policies necessarily remains in place.

or 15 per cent (reinsurance) of the risk, but the individual members of the pool are free to participate in cover outside the pool.

The benefit of the block exemption may be withdrawn by the Commission under art 17 from an otherwise qualifying agreement, in particular where the participating insurers are individually large enough to act alone, where one of the participants holds a market dominant position, where the agreement results in market division, or where the collective power of the participants makes it difficult for insurance to be obtained from any other source.

*Security devices* Article 15 permits insurers to enter into agreements which have as their object the establishment, recognition and distribution of technical specifications for security devices, including their installation and maintenance, and rules for the evaluation and approval of concerns involved in the manufacture, installation and maintenance of security devices. Article 15 lists the various conditions which must be fulfilled before the exemption applies. These require, *inter alia*, that: the agreed specifications are precise and technically justified; the evaluation rules are applied in a non-discriminatory fashion and assessments are available to all in the industry at any time; insurers are free to recognise non-complying security devices; specifications are available on request to any person; and the assessment process is operated fairly in that it does not impose disproportionate costs and it provides a right of appeal against refusal of recognition.

# Appendixes

# Dates of ratification and entry
# Convention and the

| | Brussels Convention of 27.9.68 (OJ 1978 L304/36) | | Luxembourg Convention of 9.10.78 (accession of Denmark, Ireland and the UK) (OJ 1978 L304/1) | |
|---|---|---|---|---|
| member state | ratified | in force | ratified | in force |
| Belgium | 16.2.71 | 1.2.73 | 21.8.86 | 1.11.86 |
| France | 13.4.70 | 1.2.73 | 27.2.84 | 1.11.86 |
| Germany | 30.10.72 | 1.2.73 | 7.3.84 | 1.11.86 |
| Italy | 11.8.72 | 1.2.73 | 7.5.81 | 1.11.86 |
| Luxembourg | 22.11.72 | 1.2.73 | 22.10.81 | 1.11.86 |
| Netherlands | 26.6.72 | 1.2.73 | 8.12.80 | 1.11.86 |
| Denmark | | | 27.8.86 | 1.11.86 |
| Ireland | | | 31.3.88 | 1.6.88 |
| United Kingdom | | | 7.10.86 | 1.1.87 |
| Greece | | | | |
| Portugal | | | | |
| Spain | | | | |
| Austria[3] | | | | |
| Finland[3] | | | | |
| Sweden[3] | | | | |

Notes:

[1]  Source: General Secretariat of the Council of European Union. Correct as at 13 December 1996.

[2]  The San Sebastián Convention has been approved by the Belgian parlement (although no Loi has yet been made). It is expected that it will be ratified in 1996 or early 1997. It will enter into force on the first day of the third month following deposit of the instrument of ratification.

# into force of the Brussels accession Conventions[1]

| Luxembourg Convention of 25.10.82 (accession of Greece) OJ 1982 L388/1) | | San Sebastián Convention of 26.5.89 (accession of Portugal and Spain) (OJ 1989 L285/1) | |
|---|---|---|---|
| ratified | in force | ratified | in force |
| 21.8.86 | 1.4.89 | [2] | [2] |
| 27.2.84 | 1.4.89 | 17.10.90 | 1.2.91 |
| 8.8.88 | 1.4.89 | 14.9.94 | 1.12.94 |
| 8.1.85 | 1.4.89 | 21.2.92 | 1.5.92 |
| 27.4.84 | 1.4.89 | 7.11.91 | 1.2.92 |
| 19.7.83 | 1.4.89 | 11.1.90 | 1.2.91 |
| 27.8.86 | 1.4.89 | 21.12.95 | 1.3.96 |
| 31.3.88 | 1.4.89 | 28.9.93 | 1.12.93 |
| 31.7.89 | 1.10.89 | 13.9.91 | 1.12.91 |
| 19.1.89 | 1.4.89 | 7.4.92 | 1.7.92 |
| | | 15.4.92 | 1.7.92 |
| | | 22.11.90 | 1.2.91 |

[3]  A convention for the accession of Austria, Finland and Sweden to the Brussels Convention was signed in Brussels by all 15 member states on 29 November 1996.

# Dates of signature, ratification and entry into force of the Lugano Convention of 16 September 1988[1]

|  | signed | ratified | in force |
|---|---|---|---|
| EC states: | | | |
| Austria | 26.2.92 | 27.6.96 | 1.9.96 |
| Belgium | 16.9.88 | [2] | [2] |
| Denmark | 19.9.88 | 20.12.95 | 1.3.96 |
| Finland | 30.11.88 | 27.4.93 | 1.7.93 |
| France | 14.12.89 | 3.8.90 | 1.1.92 |
| Germany | 23.10.89 | 14.12.94 | 1.3.95 |
| Greece | 16.9.88 | — | — |
| Ireland | 18.8.93 | 27.9.93 | 1.12.93 |
| Italy | 16.9.88 | 22.9.92 | 1.12.92 |
| Luxembourg | 16.9.88 | 5.11.91 | 1.2.92 |
| Netherlands | 7.2.89 | 23.1.90 | 1.1.92 |
| Portugal | 16.9.88 | 14.4.92 | 1.7.92 |
| Spain | 19.1.94 | 30.8.94 | 1.11.94 |
| Sweden | 16.9.88 | 9.10.92 | 1.1.93 |
| United Kingdom | 18.9.89 | 5.2.92 | 1.5.92 |
| EFTA states: | | | |
| Iceland | 16.9.88 | 11.9.95 | 1.12.95 |
| Liechtenstein[3] | — | — | — |
| Norway | 16.9.88 | 2.2.93 | 1.5.93 |
| Switzerland | 16.9.88 | 18.10.91 | 1.1.92 |

Notes:

[1] (OJ 1988 L319/9). Source: Swiss Federal Council. Correct as at 6 December 1996.

[2] The Lugano Convention has been approved by the Belgian parlement (*Loi* of 27.11.96). It is expected that it will be ratified in 1996 or early 1997. It will enter into force on the first day of the third month following deposit of the instrument of ratification.

[3] Liechtenstein has no plans to accede to the Convention.

# Dates of ratification and entry into force of the Rome Convention of 19 June 1980 [1]

| member state | ratified | in force |
|---|---|---|
| Austria[2] | — | — |
| Belgium | 31.7.87 | 1.4.91 |
| Denmark | 7.1.86 | 1.4.91 |
| Finland[2] | — | — |
| France | 10.11.83 | 1.4.91 |
| Germany | 8.1.87 | 1.4.91 |
| Greece[3] | 29.9.88 | 1.4.91 |
| Ireland | 29.10.91 | 1.1.92 |
| Italy | 25.6.85 | 1.4.91 |
| Luxembourg | 1.10.86 | 1.4.91 |
| Netherlands | 21.6.91 | 1.9.91 |
| Portugal[4] | 30.6.94 | 1.9.94 |
| Spain[4] | 2.6.93 | 1.9.93 |
| Sweden[2] | — | — |
| United Kingdom | 29.1.91 | 1.4.91 |

Notes:
[1] (OJ 1980 L266/1. Corrigenda are at OJ 1983 L58/14).
Source: General Secretariat of the Council of the European Union.
Correct as at 13 December 1996.
[2] These states have undertaken to ratify the Rome Convention and a convention for their accession was signed in Brussels by all 15 member states on 29 November 1996. As at 13 December 1996 no member state had ratified this accession convention.
[3] Greece acceded to the Rome Convention by means of the Luxembourg Convention of 10 April 1984 (OJ 1984 L146/1). The date of ratification shown relates to the Luxembourg Convention.
[4] Portugal and Spain acceded to the Rome Convention by means of the Funchal Convention of 18 May 1992 (OJ 1992 L333/1). The dates of ratification shown relate to the Funchal Convention.

# Implementation deadlines

SECOND NON-LIFE DIRECTIVE, 88/357/EEC
(OJ 1988 L172/1)
Implementation deadline: 30 June 1990 (being 24 months after the date of notification of the Directive to member states) (article 32).

DIRECTIVE 90/618/EEC (OJ 1990 L330/44)
Implementation deadline: 20 November 1992 (being 24 months after the date of notification of the Directive to member states) (article 12).

SECOND LIFE DIRECTIVE, 90/619/EEC (OJ 1990 L330/50)
Implementation deadline: 20 May 1993 (being 30 months after the date of notification of the Directive to member states) (article 30).

THIRD NON-LIFE DIRECTIVE, 92/49/EEC (OJ 1992 L228/1)
Implementation deadline: 1 July 1994 (article 57).

NOTE: Transitional measures may apply.

# Further reading

## General

There are a number of practitioners' texts which cover insurance law generally, and in which some discussion of all of the matters contained in *EC Insurance Law* will be found. The most important texts are *MacGillivray and Parkington on Insurance Law* (Sweet & Maxwell, new edition forthcoming in 1997); Clarke, M, *The Law of Insurance Contracts* (LLP, 1994, with 1996 supplement); and Merkin, R, *Insurance Contract Law* (Kluwer, two volumes, looseleaf, updated quarterly). The full text of all EC materials is contained in Maitland-Walker, J, *EC Insurance Directives* (LLP, two volumes, looseleaf, updated twice yearly). There are also a number of journals which cover EC insurance law, including *International Insurance Law Review* and *International Journal of Insurance Law*.

## Chapter 1: The single insurance market

The leading text on regulation is Wilshire and Ellis, *Regulation of Insurance* (Kluwer, two volumes, looseleaf, updated three times yearly). This work discusses all aspects of the detail of regulation, and contains useful summaries of EC materials.

## Chapter 2: Insurance contracts

The general works referred to are the best here, although there is a student text – Birds, J, *Modern Insurance Law*, 3rd edn (Sweet &

Maxwell, 1993) which may be of some additional assistance for an excellent summary of the law relating to insurance contracts.

## Chapter 3: Motor insurance

There is no up-to-date, specific text on motor vehicle insurance, although thorough coverage is contained in all of the general works referred to earlier.

## Chapter 4: Insurance intermediaries

There are a number of specific works on intermediaries, including Shaw, *The Lloyd's Broker* (LLP, 1996), Hodgin, R, *Insurance Intermediaries* (looseleaf, LLP, updated three times yearly) and Henley, C, *The Law of Insurance Broking* (Longman, 1990). Of these, Hodgin contains some discussion of the position within the EC, whereas the other texts are concerned with the domestic law as it applies to brokers.

## Chapter 5: Jurisdiction in insurance and reinsurance disputes

There are several commentaries on the Convention, but the rate at which judgments are being handed down means that they are often not up to date. The most readable, and perhaps the most thorough, analysis of the Convention is the invaluable *European Civil Practice* by O'Malley and Layton (Sweet & Maxwell, 1989). Peter Kaye's *Civil Jurisdiction and Enforcement of Foreign Judgments* (Professional Books Limited, 1987) also contains a great deal of information although the case law has since moved on substantially (work on a second edition is in progress). The principal English reference work on conflicts, Dicey & Morris, *The Conflict of Laws*, 12th edn (Sweet & Maxwell, 1993, with Supplement, 1996) intermingles the Convention's rules with those of the common law, but it is more up to date than the other works and is useful for reference. A less exhaustive commentary on the Convention's jurisdiction rules is to be found in Cheshire & North, *Private International Law*, 12th edn (Butterworths, 1992).

## Chapter 6: Choice of law

There are fewer commentaries on the Rome Convention than the Brussels Convention. Readers may wish to refer to *The European Contracts Convention* by Richard Plender (Sweet & Maxwell, 1991) or, again, Dicey & Morris, *The Conflict of Laws*.

## Chapter 7: Insurance and competition law

Competition law is one of the fastest-moving areas of EC law. The standard books on competition do contain some mention of the insurance materials, but are more dedicated to general principles. The leading texts are two multi-volume practitioners' looseleaf encyclopaedias, Sweet & Maxwell's *Encyclopedia of Competition Law*, and Butterworths' *Competition Law*. The best student text is Whish, R, *Competition Law*, 4th edn (Butterworths, 1996), and the best bound practitioner's text is Bellamy and Child, *Common Market Law of Competition*, 4th edn (Sweet & Maxwell, 1993).

# Bibliography

Almeida Cruz, de, Desantes Real and Jenard, *Report on San Sebastián Convention*, OJ 1990 C 189/35

Cheshire and North, *Private International Law*, 12th edn (Butterworths, 1992)

Dicey and Morris, *The Conflict of Laws*, 12th edn (Sweet & Maxwell, 1993)

Evrigenis and Kerameus, *Report on Greek accession convention*, OJ 1986 C 298/1

Giuliano, M and Lagarde, P, *Report on the Rome Convention*, OJ 1980 C 282/1

Jenard, *Report on Brussels Convention*, OJ 1979 C 59/1

Jenard and Möller, *Report on Lugano Convention*, OJ 1990 C 189/57

Maitland-Walker, J, *EC Banking Directives* (LLP, 1992)

Newman, K M, 'Background and Scheme of the Civil Jurisdiction and Judgments Act 1982' in *Jurisdiction and Enforcement of Judgments in Europe* (College of Law, 1985)

O'Malley and Layton, *European Civil Practice* (Sweet & Maxwell, 1989)

Reynolds, F M B [1994] *JBL* 265–70

Reynolds, F M B, 'Some Agency Problems in Insurance Law' in Rose (ed), *Consensus ad Idem* (Sweet & Maxwell, 1996)

Schlosser, *Report on Luxembourg Convention*, OJ 1979 C 59/71

# Index

# INDEX